Simple Successes

*From Obstacles to Solutions
with Special Needs Children*

by
Rachelle
Zola
Edited by Denise Hmieleski
Illustrated by Leah Hall and Jonathan Kidd

Outskirts Press, Inc.
Denver, Colorado

Simple Successes
From Obstacles to Solutions with Special Needs Children
All Rights Reserved

Outskirts Press
http://www.outskirtspress.com

ISBN-10: 1-59800-354-2
ISBN-13: 978-1-59800-354-3

Library of Congress Control Number: 2006921148

Printed in the United States of America

Dedication

Dedicated to my brother, Michael.
Michael, you taught me about love and
respect for myself and others.
You are my teacher.
You are my heart.

And

Dedicated to Gary, my husband, my best friend.
For 32 years you have shared with me unconditional love.
You are the magic in my life.
You are the love of my life.

Testimonials

"After many years of teaching special needs children, Rachelle Zola has taken her hands-on experience and put it into a practical, easy-to-read book. She focuses on the *can do* by providing countless concrete examples that will allow your child to experience success in learning and enrich family interactions. Her book is a must read for parents of special needs children."

Nancy Samalin, M.S., Best-selling parenting author whose newest book is LOVING WITHOUT SPOILING & 100 Other Timeless Tips for Raising Terrific Kids. She is the Director of Parent Guidance Workshops™ in New York City.

"*Simple Successes* is packed full of content in a practical and easy-to-read format. Rachelle's stories illustrate pathways to success that are inspirational and achievable. This book is a "must read" for anyone who works with people with developmental disabilities. I guarantee that readers will learn from it and be able to immediately apply the content to create even more simple successes."

Richard A. Rusak, M.S., Parent of a child who is quadriplegic, has cerebral palsy, and developmental disabilities. Retired Director of Leadership Development and Middle School Principal. Teaches sit-skiing to the disabled with the National Sports Center for the Disabled.

"As a lifetime educator, Rachelle has always shared a special bond with her students and with his or her parents. Her new book is an inspiration for all parents, not just parents with children with special needs. Her words will help anyone who wants to connect with children in a positive way. Rachelle has found a way to build that special bond with all who choose to read her book."

Robert Pantall, M.Ed., Retired Director of Special Education Programs and Services, Coordinator of Special Education Centers and Services, and Elementary School Principal.

Contents

Foreword

By Kathleen and David Egan

My son, David Egan, was one of the lucky students that Ms. Zola taught when he was at Vienna Elementary School, in Virginia, over 15 years ago. Now, David is a successful 27 years old and a staff employee at the Booz Allen and Hamilton consulting firm in McLean, Virginia. He works as a clerk in the Distribution Center, and more than just a productive employee, he is also an advocate and messenger for people with disabilities. He learned early on from Ms. Zola that the disability is not an obstacle to reaching your goals. In his public speaking, he often says, "It was hard for me to accept the fact that I have Down Syndrome, but it became easier when I found out that I was not alone. I know that I have a disability just like many others in this world but my disability does not get in the way when I want to learn. I think of all the things that I CAN DO. Thanks to my family and teachers, their patience and persistence, I quickly discovered that I CAN DO many things and my disability does not stop me from achieving my goals. I learned to use my abilities rather than to focus on my disabilities."

Simple Successes illustrates focusing on the CAN DO, on the possibilities rather than the obstacles. It personifies the way Rachelle Zola perceived her teaching role: facilitating the task, making progress even in situations where things seem impossible. One has to have an eye to see the possibilities, an ear to listen to the needs of our kids, and the willingness to act. David still remembers how Ms. Zola would challenge him and his classmates with "difficult" words. He learned not to be afraid to learn them, spell them, and use them. David's vocabulary expanded and his pride and confidence expanded too.

In another speech to the National Down Syndrome Society, David said, "Some of my teachers were particularly good because they found ways to expand my abilities. For example, Ms. Zola in 6th grade had me write storybooks and when I did not know the correct word, she would give me ADULT words and CHALLENGING words. I did not always know what they meant at first, but it felt good to use the word and get the respect of others. She did not baby me. She knew that with patience I could learn new and difficult words. Thanks to Ms. Zola, I had some experiences in public speaking early in life. I read poems at school assemblies and she had me partner with another 6th grader who was not in special education to conduct interviews in the community and write short stories that were published in the school's newspaper. And because of this experience, I was encouraged to go further and to use the media to inform the public and develop awareness about people with disabilities."

Reading *Simple Successes* reminds me of the challenging road that all parents have to walk to help our children reach their goal. It also confirms that it is possible and it just takes believing in yourself and in your child. It means that we focus on the concrete goal and find ways to making it happen.

Ms. Zola made a difference in our lives and I know she will in yours as you follow her advice. David would add, "The slow learning and unique problems that I have are no barriers to success."

Introduction

In my classroom, when one of my students would do something absolutely amazing, which happened almost daily, I'd hardly be able to contain myself. I'd want to run out into the hallway to tell everyone and I often did! When holding workshops for parents, ideas would come pouring out and the parents and I would get excited about all the possibilities. To see a child's face when he has succeeded after putting forth a courageous effort is awe-inspiring. I am passionate about the simple successes.

This book is for parents and teachers who are looking for more ways for their children to participate in home, school, and community activities. It is about what does and does not work for you and your child. It is about you being energized to look at how you are doing everyday things, and see how you might adapt what you are doing so that your child will be a more active participant in his own life.

When I tell people that I work with children with developmental disabilities, inevitably they say that I must have so much patience. It's funny because people who know me in my life outside of working with children would probably say I'm not all that patient. I'm sort of a "let's get it done now" kind of person. So instead of thinking patience, I'd like you to consider another mindset. Think about your intention. Personally, I know where the child is now and I focus all of my attention on what I want that child to accomplish. What I definitely am is tenacious; I will find a way!

As an example, do you want your child to learn to write her name? What does she do now? Does she hold a crayon or a pencil? Does she trace letters? Does she write any letters by herself? Does she use a computer keyboard? These are some of the questions you will answer before you proceed. Your intention is clear—your child will learn to write her name. Now it's up to you to keep coming up with ideas until you hit upon the solution that works for her. You are in this with her, sharing her failures and successes.

I do not concern myself with a "right" way because I'm going to suggest there is no "right" way. Instead I want you to consider what will work for your child. For me, I know the child is going to get to the finish line. I don't know *how* she's going to get there, only that she *will* get there. When you're excited and joyful about what your child is achieving, you will see a smile on your child's face that will light up the skies. There is no better feeling; there is no greater gift.

Have fun with the challenge. Do not turn this into hard work. My wish is that you will discover new and different ways to bring more independence to your child. I want you and your child to know how capable they are instead of feeling *less than, not good enough,* or *not smart enough.* As parents and teachers, it's up to us to find ways to guide them and enable their magnificence to flourish.

Remember, your child is a child first no matter what challenges he may have. This is a jumping off point. Savor the simple successes.

Part One

Holding Your Child Capable

During my first year of teaching a kindergarten/first grade class of children with developmental disabilities, I invited the parents to my classroom to meet me, get to know each other, and to see where their children were going to spend their time for the next nine months.

One of the first things I asked them to do was tell me if they thought the room looked messy or neat. They all agreed that it looked neat. I told them I was very pleased to hear that because their children had cleaned the room, not me. I then shared with them many of the things that I planned for their children to do and what they *could* do. For me, what I was saying to them came naturally with certainty and clarity. I knew we were going to have a great year, and here were some of the exciting things that I was looking forward to doing with their children.

I had not anticipated their response. They explained that for most of their children's lives they had heard only what they could *not* do. Their children had been tested and re-tested, and they just didn't meet the standards. Even though their children may have had good pre-school experiences, the parents were not getting the message that their children were okay just the way they were. Here was an opportunity to allow them to look at their children differently, to see how capable they were. It was an eye opener for all of us.

I had a parent upset with me for allowing his son to take out a library book about dinosaurs that he couldn't read. I asked the parent if his son could tell him all about the dinosaurs on the pages. The answer was yes. I asked him if his son was excited about the stories he could make up about the dinosaurs. Again, the answer was yes. If his child couldn't read the words on the page, he felt it wasn't an appropriate book.

After our discussion, he re-evaluated this way of thinking. He saw that his son was getting great value from the book and was having a wonderful time sharing his knowledge of dinosaurs. This parent went home to enjoy the book with his son.

Recognize that your child is capable and wants to learn, and together you will find a way for that learning to take place. You are creating an environment that is conducive to learning by communicating respect and having a safe space for him to make mistakes, practice, and succeed. When you believe in your child and you communicate that to him, he will believe in himself, show confidence, and be willing to take risks.

Be clear on what tasks you want your child to perform. This is not something you are "doing" to him. He must be an active participant. When speaking with him, it is extremely important to use language that is concrete. Be specific; use details that will enhance the experience. In this way, not only are you clear about the results you are striving for, your child will also be clear, and together you will achieve the goal.

It is essential for you to appreciate how much influence you have in your child's life. Your beliefs, attitudes, actions, and feelings are felt and internalized by him. How your child responds to you depends heavily on what you are communicating, both verbally and nonverbally. Children naturally trust their parents and look up to them for guidance and encouragement. Let your child know you trust him also. Be there for his failures and successes. Let him know what a splendid individual he is.

I remember staff members saying what a nice kid one of my eleven-year-old students was, and too bad he wasn't able to learn. It was true, he did not read or write when I met him, and he told me he wanted to learn. So began our journey.

I held him capable. I already knew he had the desire. We took very small steps: recognizing a sight word, learning phonic skills, and writing down the words he wanted to learn. Along the way he made mistakes and would get scared. I assured him that we were in this together, and as long as he was willing to continue, I would be right there with him.

By the end of the school year, this young boy was reading and writing at first grade level. What is significant about this is that he now saw himself differently, as smart. When we went on field trips he could read the words on signs, on labels, on trucks, and he even attempted to read words that weren't familiar to him. He was a child who could learn.

Think, Say, Do

Take a moment to look at your own thought system—what you are saying to yourself. Are you grounded in the belief (do you tell yourself) that your child is capable and wants to improve and that you can assist? Or, are you grounded in the belief that she can't do it or doesn't even care if she can't do it, so why bother? The results will be very different depending on what you are saying to yourself.

Can you think back to a time when you have told yourself one thing, said another thing, and did something entirely different? It goes something like this:

You're going to teach your child to ride her bicycle. You're thinking to yourself, *she can't ride a bicycle.* Then you tell her, "You can learn to ride a bicycle." Then you spend minimal time and effort assisting her, not giving her the time and care she needs to practice and eventually succeed. What message did your child receive? Maybe she's thinking, *I can't do this,* or *I'm too clumsy,* or *Mommy/Daddy is mad at me.*

Take a moment and think if there have been times like this that pertain to you. Be aware of your thoughts, words, and actions, and if appropriate, do something different. Remember, this is about what works for you and your child. This is not about blame or finding fault.

When working with children, I like to think that each child is telling me something. Sometimes I just haven't figured out their language yet, and I know I will. Maybe their behavior is disruptive, or I see frustration in their faces while working on a new skill. I know something is not quite okay. I begin by listening and observing again. *What did I miss? How can I change my own performance?*

I determine what I might do differently so the child can accomplish his goal, perhaps for the first time. The modifications are usually very simple. I ask myself a lot of *what if* questions such as: *What if I do...? What if I say...? What if I use...? What if I stopped...?*

I begin to make a mental list of other activities, materials, and computer software that I can use. Maybe it's as easy as playing some music to change the mood in the room. *What if I spoke in a different tone, softer, louder, in a silly voice? What if I broke down the task into smaller increments?*

How many times do I go through this process? As many times as it takes.

I was a substitute teacher in a pre-school class, and the aide for the class told me that one of the little girls always cried all day long when a substitute was in the room. (People around her saw that this always happened and expected it to happen again, which in fact, it did.) This student walked into the room, saw me, and sure enough, started crying great big sobs. At that point, I felt I had two very clear choices: to either accept the crying or do something different.

I wanted her to have a happy, anxiety-free day. That was my starting point. I was looking for a different outcome, and it was my job to find something that would work. I sat down next to her, introduced myself, and told her I was going to wrap a beautiful rainbow cape around her, and whoever wore this cape had a very happy day.

I asked her to assist me. I told her it was an invisible cape and that I was going to take my arm and make a circle around her for each of the colors. I asked her what she wanted as the first color. She hesitantly told me, "Pink." Then I said in a gentle voice, "Okay, I'm putting pink all around you. It's the most beautiful soft pink I've ever seen. Can you see it?" She shook her head yes. "What's the next color?" I asked. I repeated this until she had six or seven colors on her cape.

She had a wonderful morning with lots of laughter, and then we went to recess. At recess she began to cry again. I went up to her and said, "Oh my, you lost your rainbow cape! Let's make another one." We did, and she didn't cry the rest of the day.

A couple of months later I was in the school for another class. This little girl saw me and yelled out, "There's the rainbow teacher!" I have a feeling she still uses her rainbow cape.

This little girl was frightened, and it was my job to create a safe environment for her. Will the "rainbow cape" work for all little children? Probably not. It's our job to find out what *will* work by listening, observing, talking, and knowing that the child wants to find a solution as much as we do.

I once worked with a young girl who had severe developmental disabilities and cerebral palsy. She spent her days in a wheelchair. She was able to move her arms but was not able to hold a crayon no matter how hard she worked at it. Her hand was in a partially closed position so I knew that she could grip something. I went to several hardware stores and found the perfect pliers for the task; it had a curved grip that her hand and fingers could fit around and a round space to insert a large crayon. The next day she was drawing!

Modeling and Thinking Aloud

Thinking out loud is a wonderful way for your child to hear about a mistake you have made and how you are going to resolve the problem. He will learn to problem-solve from your modeling. He will learn that there is a process to solving problems, that there are steps to be taken. Most of us do this automatically, in our heads, so children don't get the benefit of this learning opportunity.

When you think out loud, your child gets to go through the entire process with you, taking the necessary steps. He will hear the mistake, your frustration, puzzlement, or other emotions you are feeling, witness your self-corrections, and then see the results of your actions.

For example:

- You accidentally spill something in the kitchen. What's your reaction? How do you handle it? You might say, "Oh no, I spilled the water! I get the sponge and stop the puddle on the counter. I clean up the spill on the floor and along the drawers."

HALL '04

- You're taking the groceries out of the car. A bag is heavy and clumsy to handle. Explain out loud what's happening, "Boy, this bag is heavy and awkward to carry. I'm putting one hand on the bottom to steady it and to make sure the bag doesn't rip open from the weight."

Making Mistakes and Needing Assistance

Many times children believe that they are not good enough. They see everyone else as smarter, better, or not needing assistance. Of course we know this isn't true. We know that everyone makes mistakes and can use support. Let your child see the side of you who doesn't have all of the answers.

One of my eleven-year-old students told me his mom never used a dictionary because she knew how to spell every word. I told him I knew his mother was very smart, and most likely there were words she didn't know how to spell, so she needed to use a dictionary on those occasions. He was very sure I was incorrect. I called his mother and asked her if she ever used the dictionary. She said she did. I told her what her son had said and suggested that she let him see her using the dictionary. He needed to see that she also needed assistance and that she didn't have all the answers.

Scheduling

Go over the day's schedule the night before and/or when your child first wakes up. If he uses language, have him share in the discussion of the next day's events. For example:

Parent: "Tomorrow morning the alarm will go off at 6:00 a.m. What are you going to do after you turn off the alarm?"

Child: "I'm going to make my bed. Then I'm going to…."

If your child does not use language, can he identify pictures? If yes, take pictures of his alarm clock, of him making his bed, brushing his teeth, putting on his clothes, eating. Depending on your child's capabilities, show him the pictures and allow him to arrange them in the order that the activities will occur. Assist him when appropriate. It may work best to show him one picture at a time, if that's where he needs to start. Seeing a picture of an activity, as well as verbal cues, may also aid him in performing the task more easily.

So much happens to your child from the moment he wakes up. The more information he has regarding what to look forward to, the more he can and will want to actively participate. Through trial and error you will learn how much information is enough for your particular circumstance. Wherever there is room for flexibility in the schedule, allow your child to make choices in what he would like to do and in what order. Again, this is another area in your life where you can model by thinking aloud what you do automatically. For example:

"I was going to read for a while after dinner and then call Grandma. Instead, I'll call Grandma now before it gets too late and then I'll read."

"Which would you rather do first, read the story together or go to the store?"

At the end of the day, have your child share with you something that made him feel good. It can be as simple as, "I saw a cloud that looked like an elephant," or "I sang a silly song." You may also want to share with your child something that made you feel good during the day. End the day in a positive way.

Putting in the Time

Being persistent, tenacious, and consistent pays off in a big way.

HALL '04

At the beginning of a school year (mid-August) I met with the mother of a five-year-old girl with Down Syndrome. She told me that her daughter was still in diapers, not toilet trained, and she didn't see the situation changing in the near future since her pre-school teacher had no success. I asked her if there was a physical problem and was told there wasn't. The issue was that her daughter was stubborn and didn't want to sit on the toilet.

This child was toilet trained by October. How did we accomplish this? Every day after lunch my aide or I took the girl to the restroom. We read stories, sang songs, and played games with her until she went. This was a pleasant experience and we did it consistently. Did it take time? Yes! Was it worth it? Yes! If we hadn't put in the time up front, we would have been cleaning diapers daily for many more months, and this child would not have gained the independence she was certainly capable of and desired. Now, she would let us know when she needed to use the toilet, and she was able to go to the girls' restroom by herself. She now saw herself as a "big girl."

When working with this child, I was grounded in the following beliefs: She was capable, she wanted to use the toilet by herself, and we would find enjoyable ways to make that come about.

Sometimes it's as easy as giving your child a little more time when making requests, giving instructions, and asking questions. Have you ever gotten frustrated or upset because your child didn't respond the way you wanted her to? Perhaps the information came in too quickly for her to understand. Perhaps she understood the information and didn't have enough time to respond. Here are some approaches that may change that:

Prepare the child. Before you actually ask a question, say, "Question," and wait a moment. This allows your child to focus on you. You can also say your child's name and wait a moment. Again, get your child's full attention before you continue.

Wait. After you ask the question, count to ten slowly so your child can digest the information. We often repeat questions before the child has time to take in the information and respond to it. For example, we may ask, "Where did you put your gloves?" When we don't get an immediate response, we repeat the question without even thinking about it, "Where did you put your gloves?"

Even when you are aware that you do this, there are still going to be times when you'll fall back into this habit. Trust me, I know! Do not get upset with yourself. Remember to breathe, slow down, and begin again.

The same is true for statements such as, "Get your coat." When your child doesn't respond promptly, it might be tempting to say, "I said, get your coat." It's important to give your child time to respond. Ask a question or give a statement, then wait.

Be focused, get eye-to-eye. Get down eye-to-eye with him. That may mean kneeling on one knee or sitting in a low chair. Sometimes it helps to hold his face gently so that he is focused on looking at you. Now both *his* full attention and *your* full attention are focused on each other, and he is set for success.

Give clear directions. 1) You are clear that your child actually knows what you want done, and 2) your child has agreed to do it.

> For example, you tell your child that bath time is in five minutes, and you want her to turn off the television and get ready. Your child nods. All you know at this point is that she heard you, not that she is going to turn off the television and get ready for her bath in five minutes. You can save yourself and your child a lot of upset by establishing ways for her to respond in a manner that will let you know that she heard you and will take the specified actions.

Use minimal cues. Give just enough information to get your child on the right track. Give him the opportunity to think and continue on his own. If it's a cold day and you are going outside, it may be sufficient to say, "We're going outside," and he'll know to get his coat. You might add, "What do you need to put on?" Then let him answer or run off and get his coat. **Caution: Be specific enough so your child isn't *guessing* what's on your mind.** For example, just waiting at the door and not moving doesn't show your child that you want him to get his coat. Body language alone doesn't always work. Do not assume that he knows what you want him to do.

Questions/Directions. Be careful about asking too many questions or giving too many directions at once. This can be confusing to your child. Take the time to slow down or stop. Allow your child time to process what you are saying.

Responding to Your Child's Answer

How you respond to your child influences how he will react. What message is he hearing?

I'm stupid.

I messed up.

Mom/Dad thinks I know how to do this, but I don't.

Dad/Mom will help me.

I can do it.

I'm smart.

Depending on the message your child receives, he can be open, confident, and curious, or he can be afraid, quiet, and withdrawn. When asking questions, allow for more than one correct answer. I use this technique because I want to learn how students arrive at their answers. What is their reasoning? I have them show me what they did. This allows them to open up and encourages positive participation. It also gives me an opportunity to learn and grow. They come up with answers I never thought of.

Personally, I have been in situations, either at workshops or in a class I was attending, when the instructor or presenter asked a question and had only one answer in mind. Attempting to answer would be so frustrating. I would wonder, *What does he want me to say?* Then he'd give the answer and I'd think that other people had given a perfectly good answer, and he wasn't open to hearing it. A learning opportunity was missed.

There are times when you might ask a question and get an answer that doesn't fit. If you think it can be a learning moment, an option may be to state a question that would fit the answer. "That would be correct if I had asked…."

The Time Factor

There really are situations when you are running late and you don't have the time for your child to do some activities on her own. Accept that, be gentle with yourself and your child. For example:

Your child takes five minutes to put on her jacket and you only have two minutes to spare. Don't tell her to put on her jacket and expect it to be done NOW, within two minutes. You're setting your child up for failure and an unnecessary upset.

Know that on some days you might need to assist with putting on her jacket, and on other days there will be enough time for her to do it by herself. Don't confuse "she can't do it" with "she needs more time to be successful at doing it herself," and don't make *your* frustration *her* frustration.

It's extremely important that you tell your child what's happening. Tell her that you know she's capable of putting on her coat and because you're running late, you're not able to give her the time she needs. There's no blame here. It's just what's happening at the moment.

Transitioning

Transitioning is difficult for many children. Some signals you might use to indicate to your child that it is time to "switch gears" are:

Ring a bell

Play music

Turn the light on and off

Set a timer

Hold up a hand

Touch the child's shoulder

Simply say that the activity is ending

What will work for your child? Allow him to participate in deciding what works most effectively. When you want him to do something else, consider the timing and outcome. Know what your goal is. For example:

You want your child to eat, and you want a pleasant time at the dinner table. He is watching television and you say it's time to eat. There are still five minutes left before the program ends.

What is going to work in this situation?

> If you insist that he come now, do you risk a tantrum? Can you let him know that when the program ends in five minutes, he is to be at the table for dinner? Does he nod his head? All you know right now is that he heard you. You want some acknowledgement that he has accepted your arrangement. Does he still need another cue from you when the program ends? If yes, what would be most effective?

You want your child to complete her homework. She has just been outside playing. She comes in flushed and wound up. What is going to work in this situation?

> Most likely she isn't ready to sit quietly and do her homework. What might work is a calming transition activity. This can be as simple as her lying on a floor mat where she can now play quietly by herself doing a puzzle, playing with blocks, or looking at a picture book. You might set a timer for fifteen minutes for this activity. When the timer goes off, she is settled down, ready to sit and do homework.

You want your child to practice his spelling words by spelling them out loud. He has just been outside playing and he is still highly energetic. What's going to work in this situation?

He's feeling good and you want to use that energy to your advantage. Create a game. Throw a ball back and forth between you. Throw him the ball and each time he catches it, he spells a word. When he throws the ball back to you, you spell the same word. Throw the ball back to him and he spells another word. What a great way for you and your child to engage in a fun activity practicing spelling, concentration, and motor skills.

Matching the Task

It's always important to match the task to the skill you want your child to learn. Here are some examples:

To write the number "2" the child takes a writing instrument and writes it. The task and skill go together. Writing the number "2" does not mean she can *count* to two or that when she sees "2" in isolation that she recognizes it and *says* "two." What you know at this point is that she can *write* the number.

A small five-year-old is given a quart of milk and asked to pour it into a glass. He lifts the container clumsily and spills the milk. Is it that he doesn't know how to pour, or is it that the container is too heavy for him to lift? If you handed him a *pint* of milk, would the outcome be different? If you want him to learn to pour, he must be given the appropriate tools to accomplish the task.

Your child is learning to use buttons. She can button up her doll's blouse, but when dressing herself, she doesn't button up the buttons of her *own* blouse or shirt.

Remember, it's a different action when you're facing a doll to button the blouse than when you are dressing yourself with the buttons away from you and you have to look down. Other considerations are whether the buttons are bigger on the doll's blouse and whether the buttons on your child's shirt or blouse are too small to manipulate easily.

One solution is to make bigger buttonholes and sew on bigger buttons.

Examine the steps that you take to put a button through a buttonhole:

- How do you initially hold the button?
- How do you hold the buttonhole open?
- How do you bring the button through the hole?
- Which fingers are you using?

Put gloves on and see how the activity changes for you.

Using buttons is a fine motor skill that takes practice. Break down the task so your child meets with success, step-by-step.

You want your child to see a pattern on a piece of paper and match it exactly, using cubes. She is given a picture of *half-inch* colored squares (red, blue, green, yellow-red, blue, green, yellow) on a horizontal line. She is then given *one-inch* colored cubes that match the colors in the picture.

She is asked to line up the cubes in the same order as the squares on the card: red, blue, green, yellow-red, blue, green, yellow.

(Note the different sizes between the picture of colored squares and the cubes.)

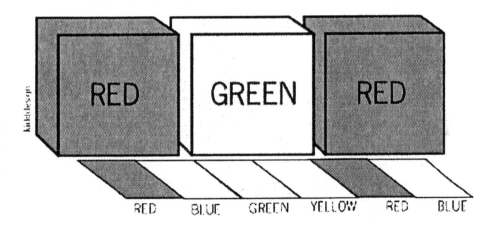

She puts the red block above the red square with the left sides lining up perfectly. She then puts down a green cube. You see that isn't accurate so you point to each colored square and ask her to give the name of the square. She says, "Red, blue, green, yellow." You think, *Great*, and you repeat the instructions. Again she puts down the red cube followed by the green cube.

Most likely, this is what's happening: When she puts down the red cube, it is larger than the picture. It covers both the red and blue square on the card, so the next color the child sees is green.

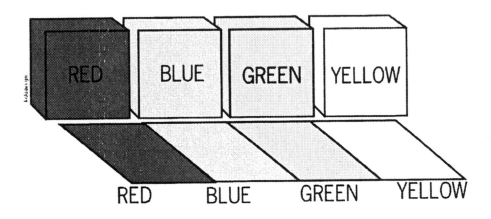

For this exercise to be effective, the colored squares and the cubes must be the same size. When the child masters this exercise, she can graduate to doing it with pictures and cubes that are not the same size.

Different Learning Styles

We all learn differently. How do you learn best? How does your child learn best? Throughout this book I ask these questions, "What is working for your child? What is working for you?" Observing your child and getting a feel for your child's learning style will make it easier for you to create opportunities for him to express himself fully.

It is important to reach every child, no matter what their learning style. Take a moment to write down how you learn best. Write down how you see your child learning best. Perhaps you learn in a variety of ways. Perhaps your child learns in a variety of ways.

An example: I'm not a strong auditory learner; I don't learn much when someone is just speaking to me, giving me information. If I'm at a seminar or a workshop I bring my tape recorder and tape the speaker. I don't take written notes easily. I'm still writing down information from the first idea I want to remember, and the speaker is onto another topic, which is very frustrating! I transcribe the information I recorded and read it. I read it as many times as I have to, to finally absorb the information. I will most likely do this by myself, away from any distractions. I also like to be "doing" an activity instead of someone showing me the activity.

Another example: My husband enjoys math, crossword puzzles, word games, and languages. When he was a young man he studied computer programming and was a "natural" at it. He is someone who sees patterns and likes to experiment and manipulate items.

Do you have a child who is intrigued by patterns? Does she put items in an orderly manner? Does she see the pattern in sentences such as, *The cat sat on the hat?* Take advantage of this knowledge when creating learning opportunities for your child.

Some children learn by manipulating, touching, and moving.

When shown the number "2," one of my six-year-old students with Down Syndrome could not give you its name. At first glance, a person would think he didn't recognize the "2." Through trial and error I learned that, in fact, he did. He needed to trace the number first, and then he could tell me what it was. He needed to get physically involved to learn.

This same child had exceptional linguistic abilities. He spoke two languages. Being from Argentina, his first language was Spanish and his second language was English. I would always marvel when we'd go into the cafeteria and he would sit with the sixth graders. He sat there because one of the boys only spoke Spanish, and this six-year-old student was his translator.

Notice if your child learns by hearing, saying, and seeing words. Does he enjoy being spoken to, reading books with you, listening to tapes, and writing? Does he love to tell stories? Use this information to assist your child in learning.

Remember, hold your child capable. You never know what wonderful surprises await you!

Many children learn through music and rhythm. Is this something your child can use as a learning tool? You might sing a song, tap out a beat, hum, or whistle. Have music playing in the background while your child is doing homework or other chores. If you observe that music is a relaxing element for your child continue experimenting. I have had students working at their desks with headphones on listening to music. Perhaps your child would enjoy playing an instrument.

Singing words was a favorite in my classroom. It was always fun and the students had great success when I used music while teaching new vocabulary. I often became a "conductor" and with each movement of my "baton" I sang a syllable. My voice would fluctuate from high to low to make each syllable distinct. All of the children would then sing the word with me. We'd sing the first syllable until everyone sang it correctly, then we'd sing the second syllable, and then we'd put the first and second syllables together. If there was a third syllable, and many times there was, we would then sing the third syllable. Finally, we'd sing the entire word. Each child also got a chance to become the "conductor" and review the new vocabulary word. They never tired of singing and learning "big words."

Here is another example of a child who learned best when able to manipulate, touch, and move:

One of my six-year-old students would stay at her desk working productively as long as she was able to stand on one foot and bend her other leg with her knee on the chair. If someone insisted that she sit on her chair for a long period of time, she would get frustrated and agitated and eventually she would cry. Here was a child who needed to be allowed to have some movement in order for her to be physically, emotionally, and mentally ready to learn.

To me this is not only an acceptable solution, more importantly, it is a healthy one. Personally, I've been okay with children moving around the classroom as long as they weren't disturbing others. Throughout this book we are looking for solutions that work for you and your child so that your child can be successful.

This child enjoyed all kinds of physical activity. I would provide her with as many opportunities to tinker as possible. I involved her with hands-on activities. A child like this may like to dance, role-play, and play sports.

Perhaps your child tends to learn better through pictures and colors. You may notice him entertaining himself with painting and drawing. He may enjoy watching movies, videos, using maps, and charts.

One of my students loved to draw and paint brightly colored pictures. I would ask her to describe her drawings and at that point she would use her language with exquisite expression. She would give every detail involved in her masterpiece, creating a wonderful experience for both of us. Through the use of visuals she was able to develop her language skills.

This same child also enjoyed working with others, sharing activities, games, and reading together. She was at her best working cooperatively.

There was a young boy in this same class and he was just the opposite. He learned better when he could be off by himself, quietly doing his projects. The other children were a distraction for him. At home this child might enjoy a private place to call his own.

Observe your child. Does your child accomplish more or seem more relaxed when in a group or when alone? Other factors to consider - what is the environment and who are the people in a given situation?

When children can hear, see, and experience something, they will retain it for a much longer time. It makes a positive difference to get them physically involved. When the experiences are a part of their lives, they will retain information and transfer the learned skills to other tasks.

In my class of students, ages eight to twelve, I did a unit on crickets. I brought a live cricket to class. I read a book about crickets to develop their curiosity. We had a discussion to build on prior knowledge. They watched a movie about crickets. They assembled a paper puzzle of a cricket to recognize the body parts. They did a worksheet on cricket habits, body parts, and contents of the cricket homes they were going to make and why the contents were necessary. The students prepared the cricket homes and put the crickets in their homes. They wrote and drew about crickets in their cricket journal and shared their journals with each other.

The students were totally involved throughout the entire cricket unit, having fun and learning. When children are laughing, sharing, playing, being challenged, and totally engaged they are full of energy; they are full of life.

In this case I didn't have any students who needed quiet time—time to be by themselves. If I had, that child would have had the opportunity to leave the group for a while and then return.

These same children learned about electricity through experimentation. They had half the classroom floor covered with wires, small light bulbs, bells, and switches. Through trial and error they learned how to make a circuit with lights going on and off and bells ringing. They learned by doing.

They also made their own birdhouses out of wood while learning how to use and store the necessary tools. Giving them the opportunity to experience learning through real life situations allowed them to use their creativity and learn problem-solving techniques.

Demonstrating New Learning

Give your child as many opportunities as possible to demonstrate her new skills. She wants to improve and she will when she is in a safe environment where she is respected. It's through practice and making mistakes that we all increase our competence. In this process, your child is setting goals with you and she will have met the goals when she can demonstrate the new skill.

Whenever a student learned a new skill, I would brag about it to everyone who was involved with the child. I always let the adults, who knew my students, know that I wanted my students to show off their skills to others. This worked out well. The children saw themselves as special and each time they performed their skill in front of new people, they felt pride and gained confidence.

If your child is learning to count, have her count cars, windows, fingers, pictures, cards, steps, cracks, houses, and whatever else she sees. She will be so proud of herself. Let her *show off* to anyone who will listen with respect.

Resist the Impulse to Redo Things Your Child has Done

How often have you received your child's artwork from school and you knew he did not do it? Do you ever "fix up" your child's artwork? It's important to allow him the pleasure of creating. Will he ever need assistance? Of course, and by allowing him the freedom to be himself, he will appreciate what he can do. The sky does not always have to be blue. Have you ever woken up before the sun has risen and watched the sky turn from black to purple to pink? I have. So, what color is the sky? Any color you want it to be.

If a child is getting frustrated and wants assistance, that's something else. However, redoing a child's work because it doesn't meet your standards just invalidates his work. He learns nothing from your actions, and if anything, will feel less worthy. Think back to a time when someone invalidated your work.

With the different special needs models in the schools, teachers are sometimes confused about what's acceptable. They may need to hear that you know that your child will not always be producing work that has the amount of detail and/or accuracy as the other students in the class and that it is okay. Have a conversation with your child's teacher giving them permission to not doctor up his artwork.

I often give this example, and I always get a knowing nod from parents. How often have you remade your child's bed after she has made it? What message are you sending if you do this? Remember to hold your child capable. She may never be able to make the bed the way you do, and when you're okay with that you will see your child grow and have her own successes. Keep in mind that children want to do well.

Compliments and Praise

Give compliments that are appropriate to the situation.

The first time your child accomplishes a task, there will be much excitement and specific praise. For example:

"Fantastic! You put your coat on all by yourself and zippered it too! I'm so excited for you and I can see how proud you are from your wonderful smile! Yes! High fives!"

When your child does it again, there's still excitement—just not the same intensity, and when he has mastered the task, there is no need for a compliment. If someone complimented you for putting your clothes on correctly when you've been doing that by yourself for some time, how would you feel? What would you be thinking? Would you be insulted? Would you be thinking that they aren't really paying attention to you? Would you be thinking that they aren't holding you capable?

The purpose of changing your level of excitement is to meet the needs of your child. In some cases, you want your excitement level to remain high. For example, when I was working with a young boy with severe developmental delays who was blind and had cerebral palsy, he loved to hear the excitement in my voice every time. It didn't matter if he threw a ball to my dogs or picked up his spoon to feed himself, he laughed with glee when I told him how wonderful he was.

<u>Be specific in your praise and compliments</u>.
For example:
> "The purple and yellow in your picture makes me want to dance."

Maybe your child doesn't share his toys and you see him sharing. Say, "Sarah enjoyed playing with you and your blocks. You were very thoughtful to share."

"Rachel, I love your picture. I like the way the roof comes to a point, and the color red around the windows makes the house appear cheerful. I would like to live there."

Your child hears that the praise is genuine. It's much more effective than only saying, "What a great picture." If you make a habit of saying, "What a great picture," each time she draws a picture, your child will not believe you for long. She will think it's just something you say with no special meaning attached to it.

Being specific allows you to give compliments freely without worry. When I was teaching, there were times when children would call me to their desks to show me their magnificent drawings. They were sure I would recognize what it was, but I often didn't. It always worked out well because I would describe what I saw, such as the colors and shapes, and they would tell me about their drawing. What was important was that I recognized the effort they put into their drawings. I showed that I cared by being specific and noticing the details that were important to them.

Catch your child doing something well.

For example:

"You did a wonderful job brushing the dog. She looks so pretty now."

Give praise at the appropriate time.

For example:

Your child is five years old and in the process of toilet

training. He's playing with other children in the park and you say aloud, "You must be so proud of yourself! You haven't wet your pants today!" In this example, the praise is not appropriate for the circumstances. This can only set up your child for ridicule and teasing by the other children. If you were alone with your child this praise would have been appropriate.

Do not give praise for something done incorrectly.

Your child will recognize this and nothing productive will come of it. People who do this may think they are being kind, when in fact they aren't holding the child capable, and there's nothing kind about that at all. The mistake many people make is to think the child doesn't know that she isn't as smart as her brother, sister, friend next door, or some of the children at school. She knows, and it's okay as long as you hold her capable and you are honest with her.

It's the same as telling me what a great dancer I am when I'm struggling to do some basic steps without tripping over my partner's feet. The truth is, I'm not a great dancer, and you haven't done me any favors by saying I am. Hold me capable. Encourage me. Let me know that I'll learn to do the dance step. I'm just not there yet.

Why Can't I?

Acknowledge your child's frustration and anger when he sees a sibling doing something easily that he has been struggling to learn. Don't dismiss what he is observing. What he sees is fact. Give him credit for seeing the difference. Depending on the severity of his disability, he will see that his brother or sister is riding a bicycle and he's still riding a tricycle.

Your child knows that his siblings are reading books and he isn't. Many children with developmental disabilities are smart enough to know that they are not as smart as their brother, sister, mom, dad, or friend, and it's important for you to know that. Too many times adults dismiss their children's concerns, anger, and frustration, thinking they are not aware enough to notice the differences. Not true!

My husband, Gary, and I were living in Colorado when my father invited Gary to work at his plumbing supply company. We moved to New York and Gary started working at the store. He quickly learned the inventory, customers, pricing, buying, and selling.

My younger brother, Michael, who has a developmental disability, had been working at the store since he was a kid and now he was 20 years old. Gary was 27. Michael saw immediately what Gary was accomplishing and he was jealous, frustrated, and angry. He wondered why Gary was doing so much more than he was. He had been there for years, and he was still basically doing the same thing— putting away the inventory. It was a very painful time for Michael.

Gary spoke to him and explained what Michael already knew— that Michael learned at a slower pace. Gary also let him know that there were many things that he could do.

It was also a painful experience for Gary. For the first time he truly felt how frustrated and aware Michael was of his inability to pick up many of the basic skills that Gary took for granted. Before this, Gary assumed that Michael did not notice the differences in their capabilities or that he did not care. He also had never had any sense of jealousy from Michael. He knew Michael wanted to be a man, wanted to be one of the guys, wanted to be confident. He wanted to be just like Gary.

It was a difficult situation for both of them to come to terms with emotionally because outside of work, socially, it wasn't about I.Q. and it wasn't about who could do more—it was about being with each other and enjoying each other's company.

Thirteen years later, having moved back to Colorado for a while, we made another move—this time to Virginia. Michael was now 33 and Gary was 40. Although confident when it comes to business, numbers, and computers, Gary felt very lacking when it came to anything mechanical or repair related. We still hadn't hooked up the dryer when Michael and his family came to visit us in our new home.

Gary was telling Michael that the plug for 220V in Virginia was completely different from what he was familiar with in Colorado. Michael walked into the utility room, looked at the dryer plug, and with total confidence in his voice explained to Gary what part was needed to fix the dryer. They went to the store and got the part. Michael then changed out the connection to the dryer and plugged it in. It worked perfectly.

Michael had taken for granted what he could do, not unlike many of us from time to time. He was matter-of-fact with no bravado and no visible special pride in what he had accomplished. He definitely displayed the attitude of let me fix this, and then we can move on to doing something fun. Here was something Michael could do easily that Gary could not.

Gary learned a huge lesson that day. Even though he loved Michael unconditionally, at that moment he realized that he wasn't holding Michael capable because he hadn't really believed that Michael could fix the dryer. He has not made that mistake again.

Another example of when adults dismiss a child's knowing is when the adult talks about the child in her presence. Please do not speak negatively to others in front of your child, especially when discussing what are considered to be her deficiencies.

Too many times I've heard teachers and parents discussing students within their earshot. Your child might not comprehend every word you are saying; however, she does pick up the meaning of the words by the tone of your voice, your attitude, and your body language. I also suggest that you interrupt someone else if you should witness this. You will be glad you did.

Being Specific

When speaking, put details into your questions and statements. The more specific you are, the more opportunities your child will have to learn. Of course, how specific you get depends on your child's abilities. Here are some examples:

"Bird."

"Look at the bird."

"Look at the pretty bird."

"Look at the pretty blue bird sitting on the fence."

"Do you want to wear the red or white T-shirt?"

"Do you want to wear the red teddy bear T-shirt or the white T-shirt with the rainbow on it?"

When exposed to a wider vocabulary, your child will begin to use that vocabulary. He will begin to model your sentence structure and will become more observant.

Speaking Out Loud

When you are with your child, make an effort to speak out loud. This is a wonderful way for children to play and learn.

Here are just a few samples of things to say and do while taking a walk:

"Feel how rough the red bricks are on this building."

"How many cracks can we step on? Let's count them."

"I'm taking three giant steps. Now I'm going to take two steps backwards. Your turn."

"Let's walk slowly, now fast. Stop! Let's jump three times. Stop!"

"Swing your arm above your head in a large circle."

"What's that sound?" (fire truck, baby crying, motorcycle)

"I'll race you to the stop sign."

"Look at the blue bird in the tall tree. Hear the bird singing."

"What colors are the leaves? What season is it when the leaves are just starting to grow?" (Don't say this all at once. Let your child observe and respond.)

"Raise your right hand toward the sky. Put your left hand on your hip and wiggle as you walk."

"The grass is green and the blades are narrow and flat. What can you do with a blade of grass?"

Remember to give yourself permission to play and laugh. Imagine all the things you and your child can experience:

Colors

Body parts

Direction/position (up/down, out/in, front/back, behind/in front of)

Quantitative concepts (little/big, thin/fat, few/many)

Numbers

Gross motor skills

Reading

Speaking

And the list goes on...

Breaking Down Tasks

It's my job to find a way for a child to learn a skill, to become more self-sufficient. One of the ways I do this is to break down tasks to the smallest denomination. This is both challenging and fun.

When I was teaching younger children, some of them had difficulty getting the paper towels out of the dispenser. They would pull at the paper towel and it would either tear or get stuck in the dispenser. I studied the action of getting a paper towel out of the dispenser in slow motion. This is what I discovered; if you first pull down with both hands, then push back and then pull down, still with both hands on the paper towel, the paper towel comes straight out without any problems. I demonstrated each of these steps to my students and they were able to grab a paper towel successfully.

HALL '04

While playing with the student I mentioned earlier who was blind with cerebral palsy, I came to realize that he could learn to feed himself; maybe not without assistance, but certainly he could partially feed himself. Up to this time an adult had always fed him. He did not participate in the feeding process at all. So how did I come to this realization? While playing with him one day, I placed a baseball cap on his head and he took it off. I placed the cap on his head again, and again he took it off. This told me that he had enough control of his arm/hand motion to grab a specific item from a specific location on his body.

I figured that if he could find his head consistently, he could find his mouth. I placed a small piece of tape on his lips and to my great joy he grabbed the tape and removed it from his mouth. Step one was complete. He could locate his mouth without difficulty.

The next step was to find a spoon or to make a spoon that he could hold firmly. Did he need a larger handle? Did it need to be weighted? Did he need the spoon to be attached to his hand? As it turned out, he was able to use a small plastic spoon that he held by himself. He would bring the spoon down to the plate, I would assist in scooping up some food, and then he moved the spoon up to his mouth and fed himself.

Here was a wheelchair-bound child who never had to do things for himself. Now every time he brought a bite of food to his mouth, he would bounce around in his chair excitedly because he had a taste of independence!

Rules

Rules can work for us or not. Sometimes we don't even know why we do them, they've just become habit. Start to notice why you do things. Is it the way that works best or just the way you've always done it? In many cases, what works for you will not work for your child.

For instance, how do you put on a pillowcase? I open up the pillowcase, put one end of the pillow into the opening, and "bounce" the pillow into the pillowcase. I've never even thought about doing it another way. This is how I've always done it.

So what is another way to put on a pillowcase? Turn the pillowcase inside out. Put your arms into it and grab the two inside corners. Still grabbing the two corners of the pillowcase now grab two corners of the pillow. Slip the pillowcase over the pillow and pull it over the entire pillow.

What other ways are there to put on a pillowcase? Which way would work best for your child?

Mutuality

Be willing to let go of your point of view as the "truth." Realize that the other person sees their point of view as "truth" also. These viewpoints are valid, just not the entire story. I consider mutuality different from compromise.

Compromise, in many cases, doesn't resolve an issue in the long term because neither of you will really be satisfied with the solution.

You may say to yourself, *Okay, it's better than nothing*, or *Why did I agree to that?* You then become resentful or if you feel that you were forced into a compromise, you may even be planning a way to get even.

Listening for mutuality allows the conversation to continue until a third possibility is created that works for all parties. There must be a willingness to trust that you will come up with a solution that works for all involved. The issues can be big or small and that also depends on how you view the situation.

For example, your daughter wants to keep her hair long— down to the middle of her back. You want her to cut it short because you see that she has difficulty shampooing it by herself. She leaves soap in her hair, and you end up brushing out all the knots. Can you mutually agree to shorten her hair to a length she can manage brushing herself and teach her strategies to get the shampoo out of her hair?

Then you have the reverse of the above example. The mother wants to keep her daughter's hair long because it's so beautiful and the daughter wants it shorter so she can take care of it herself. What is mutually agreeable? What works for you and your daughter?

This book is about doing things differently so that your life and your child's life work in harmony. I think many parents are working too hard and feeling overwhelmed. My wish for you is that you will see new ways to approach situations that will work for you and your child.

Part Two

The Kitchen and Independence

It makes a world of difference for a child to be able to prepare her own food. I've seen a child's face light up because she could peel her own banana, unwrap a candy wrapper, or open a milk container while the other students cheered her on. There is nothing better for me than seeing children hold themselves capable and achieve these successes.

The kitchen is not only a fun place for children of all ages, it is also a place to learn about independence. When I was teaching, my students and I cooked, learned a lot, and laughed a lot. We made delicious meals, snacks, and drinks with the use of a blender, toaster oven, electric skillet, and the microwave in the teachers' lounge.

My students would get so excited when they made and ate their own meals. What can be more delicious than French toast or mixing together a tuna salad, putting it on a cracker and eating it, or making pizza on a muffin in the toaster oven! Being able to prepare a meal—even the simplest of meals—gives children a sense of freedom. They develop the power of choice and learn to give themselves permission to risk. It's a leisurely activity that adds such value to their lives.

The skills your child learns in the kitchen will flow into every area of his life. Remember, hold him capable because he wants to learn, and he wants to be independent.

A Can't-Do Attitude is the adult looking at situations as obstacles and getting stuck. Here are some obstacles you might see as preventing your child from being independent:

- Quart or half-gallon milk container (too heavy, too bulky).
- Milk on shelf in refrigerator (too high).
- Glass/china bowl (breakable).
- Can't reach spoon (too high).
- Cereal box (too bulky, too big, can't hold).
- Spills (can't do it right).

- Puts too much food on plate (ends up wasting and throwing out).
- Dishes (can't reach, breakable).
- Utensils (can't touch knives—will hurt self, can't reach).
- Doesn't know where anything belongs.
- Doesn't know how to set the table.
- This is my kitchen.

A Can-Do Attitude is about the adult and child looking for solutions.

- Put milk into a pint-sized or smaller container that is light enough to lift and easy to handle.
- Put the exact amount of milk your child will need into the container so when he pours there is no chance of overflowing.
- Place the milk container on a lower shelf that your child can reach.
- Use a plastic bowl or other non-breakable bowl.
- Put a step stool in the kitchen so your child can use it to reach the drawer and take out a spoon.
- Buy the small, individual cereal boxes or put the cereal into a smaller container.
- Have your child place the bowl on a tray with a lip on it before pouring the cereal and milk. Now if your child spills the milk, it won't spread from the countertop to

the floor. It will stay on the tray, which is easy to clean.

- When cleaning up spills, show your child how to do it. Will you use paper towels, a sponge, or wet cloth? Which item works best? Show her how to wring it out.

- When there's a spill, make a game out of it. Say, "S-q-u-e-e-z-e," stretching out the word and using a funny sounding voice.

- Determine what portion of food you're comfortable giving your child. Put that amount into a container she can easily handle. Have her participate in this activity. What's too little? What's too much? What's just right? Ask yourself these questions: *Is it that she isn't able yet to judge what's an appropriate amount for her appetite? Is it that the utensils she's using are too big and clumsy for her to handle, so she isn't able to scoop out what she wants? Can she handle the containers easily?*

- Give children a "child" sized plate. Food looks "bigger" when viewed from a child's point of reference at the table. For example, if they are sitting on a chair meant for an adult they see the food from a different angle and it looks "bigger."

- Put knives in a different location so your child won't be harmed.

- Can your child put items in the sink, on the counter, or other location that is easy to reach?

- Show your child how to organize the dishwasher.

- Have your child assist in putting food away after you've gone grocery shopping.
- Examine your attitudes about the kitchen. If your goal is to have your child become independent, the kitchen is a fantastic place to start making that happen. It's about finding the tools that work for your child. When you find the tools you will see many more successes.

From these few examples, your child can now make his own breakfast and feel terrific about this new ability-and you can sleep in!

Singing, Music, and Sounds

Singing is always fun. Sing when you're cooking. Use a tune your child knows. Does she know and enjoy singing *She'll Be Coming Around The Mountain?* If yes, make up words and sing:

> "We're cooking potatoes, yes we are. We're cooking potatoes, yes we are...."
> "We're washing the dishes, yes we are...."
> "I'm mashing the potatoes, yes I am...."

What other songs does your child enjoy singing? Improvise, make up your own words.

Experiment with background music such as pop, classical, jazz, and rock and roll. Your child may or may not enjoy the music. For some children the music is relaxing, for others it is stressful. What is it for your child?

Children enjoy different sounds and noises:

- Click your tongue while stirring. Change the sound of the click by changing the shape of your mouth.
- Whisper sounds/noises and then get progressively louder.
- Hum while walking around the kitchen.
- Whistle.
- Tap out different beats just for the fun of it.
- Give a "drum roll" to prepare your child for the next step in whatever activity you are doing.
- Sing out a new vocabulary word such as "avocado." Sing it with high notes, sing it with low notes, sing it fast, sing it slow. Most of all, have fun!

Sandwiches

What rules do you have around sandwiches? Do they work for your child?

Rule: He can't make a sandwich because sandwiches should be cut in half, and he can't hold a full sandwich in his hands or use a knife safely.

Revision: He can make a sandwich by putting the ingredients on one slice of bread and then folding it in half.

Rule: The peanut butter sandwich must have two slices of bread with the peanut butter between them.

Revision: Your child can take a bite of bread and then eat a spoonful of peanut butter.

Rule: Peanut butter and jelly is spread evenly on the bread.

Revision: Is this *his* rule or *your rule*? Would he be happy eating a lumpy sandwich he made by himself? If it is important to him that the peanut butter is smooth, show him how to hold the knife. Experiment with both a plastic knife and a regular knife without a sharp edge. Weight and size will make a difference for your child.

Demonstrate holding the knife. How are your fingers placed on the knife? Show him the angle of the knife against the bread. Demonstrate how to get the peanut butter onto the knife. Then have him hold the knife, placing your hand over his and doing all the actions together. When he says, "I can do it by myself," let him do it. Then go back and fine-tune the actions one step at a time. The words "I CAN" are music to your ears. Keep the momentum going. Get into a *solution* mode.

Another option for spreading the peanut butter may be using a spoon instead of a knife. Again, you are looking for ways that work for your child.

Flexibility is the key here. Keep in mind that your goal is to help your child become more independent.

Paying Attention to Details and Being Specific

Less Specific: Hand me the milk.
Specific: Hand me the pint of milk.

Less Specific: Hand me the big spoon.
Specific: Hand me the tablespoon.

Less Specific: Put the glasses on the table.
Specific: Put four glasses on the table.

Less Specific: Put the fork next to the dish.
Specific: Put the fork on the right side of the dish.

Less Specific: Get the cereal box from the shelf.
Specific: Get the cereal box from the bottom shelf.

Setting the Table

On a piece of construction paper draw a place setting with plate, napkin, knife, fork, spoon, and drinking glass and have it laminated or use clear shelving paper and do it yourself. Here are some ideas to establish a starting point for your child to set the table.

- First, find out if you child can place the items on the laminated sheet without your assistance.
- If not, you can put the laminated sheet on the table and place all the items on it except for one item, which you hand to your child and she puts it in the correct spot.
- You can graduate to having her put two items in place, then three items.
- She may then progress to putting all the items on the laminated sheet by herself.

Check to see if she can place the items without the use of the laminated sheet. If she can, great! If not, let's look at some more steps:

- Put the laminated sheet above where you would naturally place the items on the table.
- Now see if she can place the plate below the picture of the plate on the table. If she can do this task have her put the other items on the table using the laminated sheet to guide her.
- If she can not place the plate below the picture of the plate by herself, take her hand, place it on the picture of the plate, and then guide her hand downward to where you would like her to place the plate, and assist her in putting the plate down.
- You may want to put your finger on the picture of the fork and then have her move your hand to the table where the fork ought to be placed.

Play around with this. Follow your child's lead and observe what is appropriate for your child. She will let you know what is working for her.

Using the Sink

Allow your child access to the sink when you've taken care of all safety concerns. Make sure your hot water is not so hot that it will burn your child. If you only want her to use the cold water, designate it by a sign, sticker, or picture. If you want her to be able to get warm water, teach her to first turn on the cold water and then slowly add hot water until comfortable. Mark the faucets to where the temperature is comfortable. Remember, however, it is not appropriate for all children to use the sink.

Using the Senses

- **Taste:** Have your child taste the foods and spices. Is it sour, sweet, salty, or bitter? Which does he like and dislike?
- **Smell:** Have your child identify the smells while cooking. Smell the garlic, cinnamon, oregano, chili powder, paprika. Where else has he smelled these scents?
- **Touch:** Have your child touch the foods. Is it mushy, soft, tough, prickly, bumpy, smooth?

- **Sight:** Describe the foods: "The grape is small, round, and green," or "The white, oval egg rolls funny."
- **Sound:** Have your child listen for and identify sounds such as popcorn popping, dripping water, the dishwasher, the blender, or the ice maker with ice dropping into the freezer.

Quantitative, Directional, and Positional Concepts

The more often your child hears these concepts, the more he will use them in his own language.

- "The carrot you are cutting is thick. The one I'm holding is thin."
- "That can of beans is heavy."
- "The bread is light."
- "Cut the bread in half."
- "Small potato, medium potato, large potato—which one are you going to pick?"
- "There are just a few jellybeans left in the jar."
- "Put the flowers in the center of the table."
- "Move backwards a little so I can open the drawer."
- "Close the refrigerator door."
- "Open the cabinet and get the cereal from the top shelf."
- "That is very high; you have to get on your tiptoes to reach it."
- "The napkins are in the middle drawer."

Practice Asking Questions

Ask a question and then WAIT. Your child needs time to process the question and then she needs time to answer. You might ask the question, "How many eggs do we need?" After she answers, it's her turn to ask you a question. It's okay if she asks the same question you just asked. She is practicing and learning.

Practice Making Statements

You say, "There are three windows in the kitchen." Your child then makes a statement. Perhaps she will say, "There are two chairs in the kitchen," or she might repeat what you said. Either way works. Your child is practicing and learning.

Measuring

When measuring, use the correct language—1 cup, 2 teaspoons, 1/3 cup, 1 tablespoon.

- "We need 2 cups of water for the soup."
- "The recipe calls for 2 tablespoons of olive oil."
- "The pizza is cut into 8 parts."
- "Cut the sandwich in half."

Recipes

Draw pictures for the parts of the recipe your child will be helping you with:

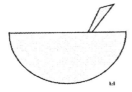

- Three eggs.
- Crack eggs.
- Put in bowl.
- Stir.

This does not have to be elaborate. Actually, I insist that it not be. White bond paper and colored markers are all you need. You and your child can both draw the pictures. You can even create your own recipe book!

Colors

Use colors to be descriptive. For example:

- "Take a big bite from the red apple."
- "The banana is mostly yellow with a little bit of green."
- "How does the green lime feel in your hands?"
- "The water is clear, and when we add a powder drink mix to it, it turns red."
- "The pan has a black handle."
- "What else in the kitchen has the color blue like your shirt?"
- "Your shirt is light blue and the blue on the can is dark blue."

Counting

You can incorporate counting into many areas. For example:

- "Let's count how many times you stir the cake mix."
- "How many eggs are in the egg carton?"
- "How many are going to eat at the table tonight? Do we have enough chairs? How many more do we need?"
- "We have four glasses on the table. If I take one away, how many will be left on the table?"
- "I can take five giant steps to get from the table to the refrigerator." (Walk and count)

First, Second, Third

Teaching your child sequencing becomes easier when you use it in everyday activities. For example:

"First, we pour the milk into the bowl. Second, we put the butter in the bowl. Third, we put in the cake mix."

"Let's make some pancakes for breakfast. Look at the pictures on the back of the box. It shows us what comes first, second, and third." Point to the number one and say, "First."

Part Three

Dressing

Here is one way that children might be taught to put on their coats: Sit on your legs on the floor. Put the coat on the floor, front facing up, sleeves spread out, and the neck opening close to your knees. Put your arms in the sleeves and pull the jacket over your head. The jacket is on. Model slowly and have your child copy your actions.

What works best when you see that your child is becoming frustrated? Sometimes a calm voice is the answer, while at other times being silly is the best solution. Children love puppets, so talking to the coat and the coat talking back is a wonderful technique to get your child laughing and playful while learning. Be silly: talk to the coat, talk to the sleeve, and talk to the zipper. "Okay coat, be still. I said be still. Stop wiggling. What a silly coat!"

Have the coat, sleeve, or zipper *talk* to your child in a funny voice. "Help! Oh no, I'm twisted up. I feel something funny coming through. Where did your arm go? Here comes your arm. I see fingers. Look out!"

Obstacle: Your child doesn't know which colors match.

Solution: Give her choices. Pick out the slacks and then give her two choices for a shirt. "Do you want to wear the red shirt with the collar or the green shirt with the three buttons?"

Remember the details: What colors are the clothes? Is there a pattern to the blouse? Does it have short sleeves or long sleeves? Is there a collar, or is it a turtleneck? Are there buttons?

Hold your child capable. Share with her that the flowered print blouse is too *busy* a pattern to go with the plaid skirt. Take out a couple of blouses that would work better. Let her pick one of them to wear.

Ask what the weather is like today. If she answers, "It's raining," hold her capable. Ask her, "What can you wear so your feet won't get wet?" After she answers, "boots," the conversation can continue. If she is going to school, will she be wearing the boots in the classroom? If not, what will she be wearing? What will she carry the shoes in? If you are taking her to the store, will she be wearing the boots in the store? Different situations, different answers.

You might have a thermometer that your child can check for outside temperature. She then can select appropriate clothes for different weather. Using a thermometer would be another way for your child to get accustomed to reading numbers. If you aren't using a thermometer, let her go outside for a moment and feel if it's cold, a little chilly, warm, or hot. Will it get warmer as the day goes on? Can she wear a sweater or a sweatshirt that she can remove when it warms up?

Obstacle: Your child can't take off his overalls to go to the toilet independently.

Solution: Have clothing that he can remove by himself. Buy pants with an elastic band. Buy shirts that he can pull over his head easily.

Remember that your goal is your child's independence. It's all right to be conscious of the latest children's fashions, and it's more important to look at what works best for your child. If buttons and zippers pose a problem, use Velcro, snaps, or even make the buttonholes bigger and sew on bigger buttons. Experiment and play.

Tying Shoelaces

I was amazed at all the different ways there are to tie shoelaces. I request that before you even begin working with your child on this task do this exercise:

Share how you tie a shoelace with another person (not someone you taught to tie a shoelace). I want you to see at least a couple of different ways to tie shoelaces so you can begin to better understand the complexity of this task if you haven't already thought about this. Have the person with whom you are doing this exercise show you how she ties her shoelace and then I want you to attempt to do it the same way. Can you duplicate it on your first attempt? Many people aren't able to.

Having the awareness that tying a shoelace is a multi-task activity will assist you in working with your child.

What do you consider your first step to be? When I've ask this question, most people say, "Making the first knot," (the knot before they start making the loops). Let's back up.

1. You pick up one end of the shoelace.
2. You pick up the other end of the shoelace.
3. You, somehow, hold the shoelace pretty evenly so that you make an "x" centered over the sneaker.
4. You push or pull one end under the "x" (I'll be calling this the "tunnel" in the below notes).
5. You pull the two ends until snug.

No problem! Right? And you've only just begun!

Wait! We haven't even talked about tightening the shoelace after we put our foot into the sneaker at the very beginning. Or maybe you had to first loosen the shoelace on your sneaker because you slid your foot out without loosening the shoelace, and now you aren't able to get your foot back in without loosening the shoelace.

You are going to teach your child to tie her shoelaces using the movements that are natural to her. You will accomplish this by listening to and observing your child. With your guidance, she will show you the best way for her.

There is no right or wrong way to tie a shoelace. Your mission is to find what works best for her. Some things to observe:

- Can she make one loop?
- Can she make two loops?
- Does she make her loops left to right or right to left?
- Does she push the lace through a loop from the front or back?
- Does she prefer using her right hand or her left hand for certain motions?
- Does she pull until snug?
- Once she pulls snugly what finger or fingers will she use to keep pressure on the shoelace so she can make the loops and have a tight finished knot?

You may want to color half of the shoelace one color and the other half another color so she can see which part she is working with. This will be especially helpful when you are talking her through the process.

Whatever works is great!

Let's look at steps 1 through 5 from above. Most adults will keep the first steps "in the air;" the shoelace doesn't touch the sneaker. What can your child do?

From my experience, most children are not able to do the task the way I do it. They do not have the fine motor skills that I have.

Here are some basic steps I use when talking through this process with children:

1. I ask them to place one end of the shoelace across the sneaker. You probably bring one end of the shoelace up and toward the middle of the sneaker. I'm asking the child to flop one end of the shoelace over the sneaker.

2. I ask them to place the other end of the shoelace over the first one.

Show them what you mean if they don't understand. Don't give them directions as to which hand to use or which end to use first. Just let your child see a shoelace flopped across the sneaker. I want her to choose and for you to observe. Does she use her right or left hand and does she go for the right or left side of the sneaker to grab the shoelace? Notice what is natural for her. If you don't see her being comfortable with her actions then assist with different hands and different sides of the sneaker. You will see the difference in her comfort level.

This may be all you do on this particular day. I don't know how long it will take your child to be able to do this much.

Note: Instead of placing the shoelace across the sneaker your child may be able to take one end of the lace and place it across the tips of her fingers and then place the other end of the lace across the first. This entire process is all about experimenting with your child.

3. Point out where the shoelace crosses to make an "x." Many children will not be able to hold the "x" in their hands.

    a) If your child can hold the "x" – observe. Is she using her thumb and forefinger? Is she using her thumb and middle finger? Remember, you want to teach her to tie her shoelaces using the movements that are natural for her.

    b) If your child can not hold the "x" in her hand, point it out and hold it up so she can see the shape it is making and the "tunnel."

4. Depending on whether she is holding the "x" or not will dictate this step.

    a) If she is holding the "x," which end is free to be moved? To make the loop under and through the "x" (the tunnel) how does she need to move that end?

Some people "push" it through with a thumb. Can she do that? Some people take the tip of the shoelace and "thread" it through the tunnel. Can she do that?

b) If your child is not holding the "x" and you are sure she sees the "tunnel," have her put one end "through the tunnel" by either lifting one end of the shoelace "over and through" or by putting one end of the lace "under and through." Remember, you want to teach her to tie her shoelaces using the movements that are natural for her.

5. Have her pull the two ends until snug. Does your child understand snug? Can your child pull until snug? Have her experiment/feel the "tension" caused when pulled.

Now continue this process throughout the entire shoelace tying task.

Note: The next step, sequentially, after pulling snugly is to put pressure on the knot. Present this step to your child and notice if she understands what you want her to do and if she can do it. If she does not understand or isn't able to add pressure, skip this step for now. After they pull snugly teach them how to make the first loop. At some point she may notice or you may point out that the shoelace is loose and her foot is wiggling around in the sneaker. Now, you can go back and add this step of putting pressure on the knot.

You will be talking to your child throughout this process. If your child is able to speak, have your child tell you what she is doing. This will also assist in reinforcing her actions.

Teach tying a shoelace, with the sneaker placed in front of her, facing the direction it would face if it was actually on her foot. It's a lot easier learning to tie a shoelace without the sneaker being on her foot because now she can comfortably move around and maneuver the sneaker without worrying about it being "attached" to her. I found that most children liked sitting on the floor with the sneaker in front of them. I also like this position because it's close to the position she will be in when she finally puts it on her foot. If you choose to put the sneaker on a table, remember, it is a very different position and view of the sneaker.

Master one step at a time. Make sure you give her all the necessary steps and do not assume that she knows all of the steps. Only when she masters each step do you teach her the next step. Get excited about each accomplished step. The adult will complete tying the shoelaces after the child has completed her last step. You want her to see the end result each time.

Experiment, listen, observe, and learn from your child. With your guidance, she will show you the best way for her. You will know what is appropriate by following her lead. For some children tying shoelaces is not an appropriate skill - in those situations Velcro and zippers work wonders!

REMEMBER:
WHAT WORKS FOR YOUR CHILD IS WHAT MATTERS!
YOU ARE LOOKING FOR SUCCESSES.

Closets

Obstacle: Child can't put clothes away because the bar is too high.
Solution: Lower the bar in the closet so your child can hang his own clothing.

Obstacle: Child can't reach the shelf in the closet.
Solution: Lower the shelf so he can reach whatever he needs.

Obstacle: Child tosses his shoes onto the closet floor creating a mess.
Solution: Put in a shoe rack to keep his shoes organized.
Solution: Get individual plastic containers for each pair of shoes for your child to place his shoes in.

Closets were not built with your particular child's needs in mind. It is up to you to make the closet functional for your child.

Drawers

Obstacle: The drawers are too heavy for her to open.
Solution: Sometimes it's as easy as changing the knobs or handles so she can have more leverage when pulling.

Obstacle: She can't put her clothes away neatly.

Solution: Put dividers in the drawer as an organizational tool.

Solution: Maybe the socks and underwear do not have to be folded.

Solution: Perhaps you can pair up the socks and she can put them into the drawer.

Please take a moment to examine your definition of neatness and the importance of neatness to you. Maybe you will find that it's really okay if she can put some items away by herself and perhaps not as neatly stacked as in your drawers, such as tossing the socks and underwear into the drawer randomly. Obviously, there are articles of clothing that when tossed into a drawer will be too wrinkled to wear. Take the time to figure out how to handle those pieces of clothing.

Storage

Obstacle: He can't put his toys away by himself.

Solution: Place toy chests and shelves low enough for him to reach.

How might you set up the room so it is user friendly for your child, enabling him to put his things away by himself? Teach him strategies.

Hold your child capable. In class, my students knew that once they finished playing with a game or toy, they had to put it away before they took out another activity.

One strategy that works well for children who have difficulty knowing where an item fits on the shelf is to make an outline of the toy or game on the shelf. Then they're able to match the item to the outline. It doesn't have to be exact; it simply gives them a place to start.

Obstacle: The room must be a showplace. Everything must be in order.

Solution: How about another point of view? The room is a safe place for your child - neat and user friendly for him.

How is the bedroom decorated? Are your child's pictures and artwork hanging on his walls? Did he help decorate it? Did he assist in selecting the paint color or wallpaper? Does he have his favorite posters hanging? Are there trophies and certificates shown around the room?

Making the Bed

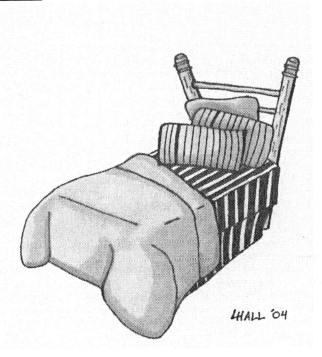

LHALL '04

What is your rule about making a bed? Do the sheets have to be tucked in with nurses' corners? Does the spread or comforter have to be absolutely straight? Do the pillows have to be in a certain position on the bed?

Is one of your house rules that your child makes her own bed? After she has made the bed, do you go into her bedroom and straighten it out without saying anything? Do you ever say, "Well done," and then go over to the bed and straighten it out? In both cases your child knows that you've gone in and redone the bed, so her actions have been invalidated. The message sent to your child is that she can't do it the right way.

Remember, there is no right or wrong way. What's important is what works for your child and you. You want her to be independent. This is her room. If you use the same standard as you use for yourself when you make your own bed, there isn't much room for her to meet with success.

What is mutually agreeable? Let's say you want the comforter on the bed. You want the sheets tucked away, but tight corners are not necessary. You want the pillows at the head of the bed close to the center. Hold your child capable. Teach her strategies for success. Is there a seam on the comforter that she can follow and place along the edge of the bed? If there are two pillows, can she put them next to each other or on top of each other? What works? You'll know it's working when you walk by her room, see that her bed is made, and you're not holding yourself back from "fixing" it.

Bathroom

Spend some time taking stock of your child's bathroom environment. Here's a quick checklist:

- Can she reach the towels without getting on her toes? Would a step stool help? Can you install a lower towel bar?
- Can she reach the sink?
- Can she reach the soap?
- Would a soap dispenser work better than a bar of soap?
- Can she easily reach the toilet paper? Can she tear it off?

- Does she know how much toilet paper to use so she doesn't clog the toilet?
- Are the toothbrush and toothpaste located in a convenient place for her use?

Obstacle: She can't maneuver a tube of toothpaste.
Solution: Have her use a pump dispenser that sits on the countertop.

Some solutions will be simple and others will be more complex. Develop different solutions to see which work best for your child and you.

Bath/Shower

Does he use a washcloth? Where is it? Where are the towels? Can he reach them?

Obstacle: He can't put the water into the tub for his bath.
Solution: Draw a line on the tub or mark it with tape so he knows how high the water can go for his bath.

Obstacle: He wastes a lot of shampoo by pouring out too much.
Solution: Ask yourself if the task matches the skill. Maybe the shampoo bottle is just too big for him to handle easily. If that's the case, buy a smaller bottle for the shampoo. For some children, the hotel-sized shampoo bottles will work great.

Is there a specific amount of time you want your child bathing? Can you set a timer? Can you put a clock in the bathroom? Is this a time for conversation, story telling, or a game? Play background music if this is something that relaxes your child.

Ownership

What belongs to your child? What decisions and choices can he make for himself? What does he have control of? Be on the lookout for opportunities that give your child a chance to experience independence. Ask yourself if it really matters, for instance, if the pillow isn't centered. If you do have some attachment to the pillow being centered, be willing to examine what it is that's holding you to that standard. By attachment, I mean having an emotional response, such as, becoming upset when the result we wanted doesn't happen and realistically can't happen. Instead of an upset, you are committed to having your child be successful in making his bed. What would that be like? When I mention holding yourself to a particular standard, I want to be clear that I'm not saying we will get rid of standards or that standards are bad. I'm saying we need to be responsible for our standards. What importance or significance does it hold for you? What are you thinking when you see the pillow askew?

I'm talking about everyday things. How do you respond? Does it matter if he decides to wear the plain white socks instead of the white socks with the green stripe? Does it make a difference which snack he eats at lunch today?

Examine your feelings and beliefs in different situations and circumstances because it is important for all children to know, without a doubt, that they have ownership for areas in their lives. When you look at these things from a different point of view, you will be able to "let go" of some things and give your child more freedom— ownership. Rather than saying, "That's the right way," or "That's the wrong way," I'm going to ask you to consider using the words, "It works for him," or "It's not working for him." How can you make it work for him? What can you do differently, not better or worse, not right or wrong, just *differently*?

Part Four

Interpretation

I'm going to suggest that you create interpretations that are gentler and more loving to you and your child when you're thinking about a situation. Maybe you're thinking, *Why can't he do the simplest of things?* Instead, appreciate what it's like for him and remember the simple things he has accomplished. Now think to yourself, *He has learned to pull his shirt over his head. What other accomplishments are awaiting us?*

When he's crying while you're working with him on a task, perhaps you're thinking, *Stop being such a baby!* At that moment allow yourself time to see the situation in another way that will give you an opportunity to be proactive. Think, *He's telling me he's frustrated.* Now, what can you say and do? Remember, you're in control of what you think, say, and do.

Generate an interpretation that brings forth compassion and forgiveness for yourself and your child. I know from experience that this will free you up to enjoy being with your child at moments when you didn't think that was possible.

<u>Chores</u>

Everyone wants to feel useful. Doing chores around the house is a wonderful way for your child to participate in family life and accept responsibility. Here are some activities to consider:

- Taking out the garbage.
- Setting the table.
- Clearing off the table.
- Vacuuming with a hand-held vacuum.
- Assisting with the laundry.
- Starting the washing machine.
- Putting soap in the dishwasher.
- Starting the dishwasher.
- Making the bed.
- Assisting in preparing meals.
- Feeding the pet.

Remember to hold your child capable and know that he wants to do it well. If you don't like the way something was done, don't rush in and fix it. Share the responsibility. Go over what needs to be done with your child and assist when appropriate.

When I was working in a classroom with multi-handicapped children ages five to seven, the adults would make a couple of trips to the cafeteria carrying the special chairs the students used when eating. Then we'd come back to the room and walk the children down to the cafeteria.

One day while we were reviewing the goals, we talked about what we could do to allow them more independence in the school. From that day on, each child pushed his or her own chair to the cafeteria. The students loved it, and they were being productive! They weren't just being taken somewhere; they got to participate in what was happening to them.

It was also wonderful because the other students in the school got to see these children being actively engaged. We all must remember to review what we're doing with children and see how we can be more effective in giving them room to grow.

Going Outside When It Rains or Snows

Go outside when it is raining and play. Let them know they will not melt.

- Dress for the weather.
- Splash in the puddles. Splash two times, now three times.
- Make big splashes and make small splashes.
- Feel the raindrops on your tongue.
- Listen to the rain falling against the leaves.

Go outside when it is snowing and play. Here are some fun things to do:

- Make snow angels.
- Make a snowman.
- Feel how soft and cold the snow is. Now make a snowball and feel how hard the snow has become.
- Poke holes in the snowball.
- Make different shapes.
- Make a snow castle.
- Feel the snow on your tongue.
- Make up a song about the snow.
- Make giant steps in the snow and retrace your steps.

Shopping

Let your child hand the money to the cashier and accept change. It doesn't matter if she doesn't count money. Interacting with the cashier is a wonderful experience. Usually the cashier will ask the customer a question such as, "Did you find everything you needed?" and your child can answer.

Create opportunities for social interactions.
For example:

- Have your child ask an employee where she might find a particular item.

- Have your child go to the deli section and ask for a half-pound of potato salad.
- Have your child ask for a taste of something on display that she might like.
- Allow her to pick out food.

Remember to hold your child capable. Let her assist you in making the grocery list. Study the store layout with her. Can she identify the aisles by the designated number and/or letter? Look for solutions. Read aisle signs. What are some items that would go in each category? Have her take items off the shelf and put them into the cart. Have her put items onto the conveyor belt when you're checking out. Make shopping an enjoyable experience with your child.

Obstacle: She doesn't know where the food items are.
Solution: Get or make a copy of the aisle directory and highlight items your child can locate in the store.

Expressing Feelings

You can start off simply with mad, sad, happy, and scared. For example:

You and your child can cut out pictures of people with different expressions and paste them on paper, making a scrapbook. Some children who don't verbalize how they are feeling can point to a picture that expresses what they are feeling.

Take turns making faces in the mirror and then describing the feeling you see. I often used a mirror in class. When children were angry (arms crossed, eyes squinted) and not acknowledging that something was wrong, I would have them look in the mirror. Most of the time they would recognize their body language and that would be enough of an opening to talk about what they were feeling.

Negative emotions can affect how a child will respond to a learning situation. If your child was fighting and then you introduced him to a new task, he might associate the fighting and the negative emotion with that particular task, and it could interfere with future learning.

It is not the best time to speak when the two of you are upset. Your child will be running on emotion, and in most cases, she will not be able to listen clearly and will likely become even more agitated. Allow time to calm down and then have a conversation.

Children of all ages love puppets. They are a wonderful way for a child to express her feelings. Children who hardly speak will put a puppet on their hand and begin talking! You can have such fun with puppets. Don't be surprised if your child takes more risks while speaking through a puppet because it will free her up. If she is upset or has a problem, have her play with a puppet and you may get the information you need to help solve the problem. They can be as elaborate or as simple as you want. Paint two eyes, a nose, and a mouth on a finger and you have a finger puppet! Help your child build a stage from a cardboard box and hang some material for a curtain.

In school, part of what we did in class was an "I feel..." activity. During the day I would have them tell me how they were feeling and I'd share how I was feeling. They would start with "I feel..." and then give a feeling. This worked well when they had mood changes during the day, and it gave them an opening to express their feelings.

Reading a Book

When reading a book, look for how this particular story relates to your child's experiences and talk about it. For example:

"What happened?" After you get a response, you can ask, "Has something like that happened to you?" If your child says no and you know of an incident where he experienced a similar situation to the one in the story, ask him some questions that may remind him of the situation. If that doesn't work, tell him about the time you're thinking of and develop a dialogue from there.

"How did the characters feel? When have you felt that way?"

"What do you think will happen next?"

This could be where you end reading for the night. You might have your child draw a picture of what he thinks will happen next. Then the next time you read, you can compare what he drew with what actually happens in the story.

He could also dictate a sentence for you to write under the picture or if appropriate, write it himself. If he can trace letters, write the sentence and have him trace over your letters. Read the sentence aloud; then have him read it aloud with you. Finally, have him read it alone.

Reading to your child, even for fifteen minutes a day, will make a positive difference. The more language he hears, the better. Read the same story over and over. Most children love to hear the same story over and over again. He will begin to recognize some words and remember what happens and in what order. He will begin to recite parts of the story to you. This is a very important and exciting time for you and your child. Your child may say that he is reading to you even though he has only memorized the story and does not recognize all of the words. He is now motivated to learn to read the words. When he's "reading" the story to you, he's holding himself capable and is very proud of this accomplishment. Smile, enjoy the moment.

Writing Stories with Repetition and Creating Books

Each page will have one thought or action and a picture to match the action. Examples of stories with three pages:

- Watch me run. Watch me jump. Watch me climb.
- Run to the swing. Run to the house. Run to the ball.

- See me run. See me jump. See me climb.
- Look at my car. Look at my house. Look at my ball.

You can add new vocabulary to new stories.

Children love having their own books, and they are easy to put together. Here's how:

1. Take blank colored or white 3" x 5" index cards, or larger, and put two holes on the left-hand side using a hole-punch.

2. Write one sentence on each card. Do not write on the back of the cards.

3. Your child can either draw a picture or you can take a picture from a magazine that matches the sentence. You might even take an actual photograph of your child doing what the sentence says. Paste the picture to the card and then laminate it.

4. On another index card, make a cover with a title for the book. Write the word author on this card, and put your child's name on it.

5. Tie ribbon through the holes or use ring binders. You'll have a wonderful finished product that your child will

love to read. These "books" are easily carried because of their small size, and of course, you can make them as big as you want.

You can make a variety of books: alphabet, numbers, days of the week, months of the year. Take pictures with a camera and then write a story about your family, your pet, your neighborhood. Remember to hold your child capable. Let her take the pictures. The bookshelves in my classroom were covered with these books and the children never got tired of reading them.

Obstacle: I have an expensive camera and I don't want her to break it.

Solution: Buy a disposable camera that she can use and don't worry about it being dropped or broken.

Obstacle: She doesn't hold the camera straight.

Solution: She's taking the picture and if you see that she's proud of what she's done, even if the picture is off center, she is being successful!

Writing Stories Using Your Child's Words

Children will remember what they dictate to you and they will be able to read it back.

As a teacher, I would take my students (ages eight to twelve) on trips to the mall, to a grocery store, to a car dealership. They knew that when we got back to school they would be writing a story about their experiences.

Because young children's verbal vocabulary is much larger than their reading vocabulary, the language in their books tends to be more expressive. They learn to read these words because they are their words, their sentences.

Ask them questions while you are writing it so the story will have a flow. Do not rearrange the "plot" because you will lose the story they wrote and they won't remember it, and if they don't remember it, they won't be able to read it.

There was an added bonus: since each child knew their part of the story, they were then able to teach the other children that part, and then all of the children would be able to read the entire book. It was magical for me to watch these children sitting around the room on the floor, reading their big books. These were children, who were not supposed to learn to read well, and here they were, reading these fantastic books that they had created. We made the big books out of large sheets of colored construction paper and then I laminated them. Besides writing the entire story, they also illustrated each page.

Children Love Words

Make charts.

Maybe you want your child to learn to recognize "L" because his name is Lonny. Begin to notice, out loud, all the "L" words: lollipop, loud, lips. Your child will start to recognize sounds in the words he is speaking. Write these words on a chart and read each word aloud. He will start hearing these initial sounds and telling you words that have an "L" in them. It will become a fun and spontaneous activity for your entire family.

Make charts for blends.

For example, start a list for "ch." Give the sound and say a word that begins with the "ch" sound, "child." Write the word down. Repeat the word. Have your child repeat the word and read it. Ask your child if he can think of another word that begins with the "ch" sound. If he can, get excited about the word and write it down. Then have him read it.

If he can't think of a word, point to a chair and ask him what you're pointing to. Get excited about the word chair. Write it down and have him read it. In time he will learn to read many of the words. Every time he says a word that begins with "ch," comment on it and write it down for him to see.

You can't always be running to the chart, so write it down on scrap paper for now and when you do have time, make a special occasion of putting it on the chart. Have him count how many words are on the list.

Pick a word for the week.

Perhaps, pick a word he finds funny to say. Look in the mirror with him to see the shape of his mouth when he is saying the word.

Teach syllables by singing the words.

Use your arms like you're conducting an orchestra, marking the syllables "won-der-ful." This is supposed to be fun—PLAY! Sing it loudly; sing it softly. Move your arms slowly; move your arms quickly. Sing in a funny voice. Catch yourself and your child saying two and three syllable words. He will join in as well. Have him notice the vibration on his lips and throat.

Children love to receive and read mail.

Write him a letter he can open at school. Send e-mails, drawings, and pictures.

Poetry

Most children enjoy and love to recite poetry. This may not seem true when you first introduce your child to reciting poetry. Don't give up. Remember, you are asking your child to take a risk. He can memorize the poem, which can be two words, one line, three lines or repeating the same sentence a couple of times. Remember, do whatever works for him.

Besides memorizing, your child learns poise and works on enunciation and pronunciation, while being expressive. Have him make a costume with your assistance when appropriate. The costume can be simple with a couple of props, or elaborate—your choice. Have him act out his poem in front of an audience and videotape the performance. Also, videotape him when he is practicing the poem. Children enjoy seeing themselves and it also provides great feedback.

Here's an example of a simple poem:

Oh, what have I done?
Oh, what have I done?
I've lost my mitten.
Oh, what have I done?
Oh, what have I done?

While reciting the poem, your child can be shaking his head from side to side. For more action, he can be holding the sides of his head while he's moving his head from side to side. He can then hold up one mitten.

You can make up your own poems or you can go to the library and bookstore to find poetry books that fit your needs.

At the end of our poetry unit, we invited all the families for a night of poetry. It still brings a smile to my face thinking about how thrilled the children were to be performing.

Erasable Boards

Children love to draw and write. Give your child as many opportunities as possible around the house. One way to do this is to have erasable boards in your home. Keep them in the rooms where you spend most of your time.

Money

Teach only **one** coin at a time. For example:

- Show your child a penny.
- Say the "P" sound.
- Say the word "penny."
- Have a jug with pennies and let her play with them.
- Count them out.
- Make designs with them.
- Build with them.
- Twirl the pennies.
- Balance them on her fingers.
- Roll pennies between her fingers.
- Toss them.
- Put a few pennies in her hand and have her shake them.
- Touch the penny. Does the edge feel smooth or rough?
- Describe the penny. What's on each side? What color is it? What's its shape?
- Draw an outline of a penny.

Suggestion: Don't put out a few different coins and ask her to pick out the penny if she hasn't mastered the penny. Once she confuses two different coins, it is very difficult to *unlearn* those first associations.

Perhaps you've had an experience similar to what I'm referring to. For example, when you met two people at the same time and heard their names at the same time. Then every time you saw them individually you weren't quite sure who was Lois and who was Louise. Maybe you tried associations—Lois has blue eyes. The next time you saw Lois, however, you couldn't remember if Lois has blue eyes—or was it Louise?

You want to anticipate confusion and avoid this circumstance as much as possible with your child. Don't have her guess the name of a coin. Give the correct answer before she has the chance to answer incorrectly. Leave the situation with her hearing the correct answer.

Most likely your child will let you know when she's mastered the penny. She may see a dime or nickel and ask, "What's the name of this coin?" Then you'll know that she can differentiate a penny from the other coins. Once she knows the penny, you can teach her the nickel. After she has mastered the nickel, teach the dime, and then the quarter.

Measuring

Have a ruler and tape measure easily available. Measure everything in the room. Measure to the nearest inch. Have a list of everything you have measured and the measurement next to it. Ask your child to do some of the writing, when that is appropriate. Teach him the symbol for "inch" and have him write the number of inches and the inch symbol.

While measuring, ask him which item is longer and which item is shorter. Remember to give him enough time to take in the question and then to respond.

Utilize the bathroom scale. Have him weigh himself in the morning and at night. Does he weigh the same or is his weight different? Is it more or is it less?

Utilize the kitchen scale. Have him weigh food items.

Telling Time

Does your child recognize numbers? If yes, you can start teaching her how to tell time. Use a large toy clock with gears for this. You can find these clocks in stores that sell educational items. Do one concept at a time. First, focus on the hour. When each hour has been mastered, you can do one minute after the hour, if appropriate.

Begin with the hour. Put the hour hand on the one and the minute hand on the twelve. Explain that when the long hand is on the twelve we say "o'clock." A great way to assist your child in remembering this is to have her raise both of her hands in the air and in a big voice say, "o'clock." I did this with children as young as five and as old as twelve and they loved it. Then show her that the short hand is pointed toward the one. Tell her the time is one o'clock and raise your hands in the air when you say "o'clock." Now have her do it with you.

Next, move the hour hand to face the two and ask her what number the hour hand is pointing toward. When she says, "two," point to the long hand that is directed upward and say "o'clock." Then have her say, "two o'clock," again raising arms in the air.

Play around with this. Shout out "o'clock" when you raise your arms. Wiggle around when you raise your arms and say, "o'clock." Have fun and learn at the same time. Move on to three o'clock and then maybe back to one o'clock. Allow your child to move the hands. Have her ask you what time it is. Always give the correct time. You do not want to confuse her.

When using an actual clock, use one with a large face and a second hand. With your child, watch the second hand go around and around. Count the seconds. Watch the minute hand move. Count the minutes. Does she recognize when a minute has gone by? Introduce the word "past." Now you are ready for the next step.

I suggest starting with one minute past two o'clock so there isn't an opportunity for your child to get confused with the ones. One minute past one o'clock might be confusing. Now watch as the minute hand starts moving away from the twelve. You can say, "Good-bye two o'clock," using hand gestures and waving good-bye to the clock. Say, "It is now one minute past two o'clock." Then set the clock to three o'clock and repeat the process of saying good-bye to three o'clock and saying, "It is now one minute past three o'clock." Remember to work with only one concept at a time.

Our children are so fortunate to have technology available to them. They can use digital watches if that works better for them. Also, not all children will be telling time and that is perfectly okay.

Remember to use the correct vocabulary of morning, afternoon, or night. "It is eight o'clock in the morning," or "It is eight o'clock at night."

Quantitative Concepts

Here are the concepts you and your child can work on.

little/big	slim/fat
few/many	thick/thin
light/heavy	narrow/wide
short/long	least/most
shallow/deep	small/medium/large

You do not need a structured lesson for your child to learn these concepts. When you are walking down a hallway you can say, "This hallway is wide. We can walk next to each other and not even touch the walls," or "This hallway is narrow. It's too narrow for us to walk next to each other."

Put a big and little ball in each of his hands. Can he pick out the big ball? Can he pick out the little one?

Have your child close his eyes. Put a big and little ball in each of his hands. Can he pick out the big ball? Can he pick out the little one?

Have him compare other objects. Which is heavier or lighter, or are they the same weight? Which is thicker or thinner or are they the same? Say, "Find something in the kitchen that's heavier than this apple," or "Let's weigh these two apples. Which is heavier?"

Directional and Positional Concepts

up/down	center/corner	through/around
closed/open	high/low	off/on
go/stop	beginning/end	inside/outside
far/near	below/above	front/back
toward/away	coming/going	straight/crooked
right/left	here/there	over/under
forward/backward	right/middle/left	top/middle/bottom

You do not need a structured lesson for your child to learn these concepts. When you are walking outside you can walk forward, you can walk backward. Make up games having your child hold items. Say, "Hold the paper above the table; now hold the paper below the table." Make up games having your child place items. Say, "Place the piece of paper near me; now place the piece of paper far away from me." Then have your child give you directions. She may repeat exactly what you said or she may come up with new directions. Remember, you are looking for what works for her.

Right/Left

When you are first teaching right and left hands, it's a good idea not to be facing your child when identifying your right and left hands. This can be confusing to her since your right hand will be opposite her left hand and your left hand will be opposite her right hand. It may never be appropriate to be facing her when demonstrating right and left. Personally, I prefer people to be next to me or in front of me, facing the same direction I'm facing, for example, when teaching me a dance step.

Outline her right and left hands on paper and then cut them out. Put the right-hand cutout on your refrigerator or some place within easy reach. Tell her to find her right hand by having her match it to the cutout. Once she has mastered the right hand, put up the left-hand cutout.

Sorting and Classifying

Here are some ideas of things you can sort and classify:

- Things to drink: juice, milk, soda pop, water.
- Things to eat: apples, cereal, banana, hamburger, cheese.
- Animals: What is the same, what is different?
- Eye color: Look for people with blue eyes, hazel eyes, brown eyes.
- Cars and trucks: Two doors, four doors, three doors, hatch back.

Junk Boxes

Things to put into a container:

keys	key chains
shells	paper clips
magnets	bells
small blocks	checkers
coins	small plastic toys
any other small items	

The container can be a box, can, plastic milk cartoon, or anything else that is easy to handle. You can make a game out of making different patterns with all the items. Your child can copy your design and then make his own patterns for you to copy. The items are fun to touch with all the different textures.

Have your child take out some keys and line them up from smallest to largest.

Have your child put the keys into different patterns.

Have your child count the keys.

Have your child put the keys into groups: two keys, three keys, four keys.

You get the idea. Repeat this process with the other items.

Following Directions

Begin with one direction and slowly build from there. Keep in mind that you are looking for successes. Give your child enough time to process the information. Have her repeat the direction. You will get great feedback from doing this. You will learn if she heard it correctly or not. If she heard it correctly, does she understand what to do? Model the directions for her if she doesn't know what to do.

The directions do not always have to be verbal. You can give directions using verbal cues combined with written cues as well as picture cues. What works for your child?

I tutored one teenage boy with severe developmental disabilities who met with success once I put the directions in writing and numbered them. All of a sudden, the idea of doing these things in order made sense to him. He needed to see it written down: 1, 2, 3. I didn't think to write down the directions and number them right away because he could only read a few words. As it turned out, writing down a few words and numbering them was exactly what he needed to meet with success. So, why did I do it? Because I was looking for solutions and that was one more thing I could do differently and see what the outcome would be.

For another child, I drew simple pictures that he was able to refer back to while following the directions. Teach your child to check off what he has accomplished. Experiment, play, and learn from all of your approaches.

Writing

Suggestion: Don't teach "d" and "b" and "p" at the same time. What was true for learning the names of coins holds true for these letters. Once a first association has been learned, it is very difficult to unlearn it. Have your child master one letter at a time to avoid confusion. Watch how he forms letters. What works for him? His hand coordination is not like yours, so don't expect him to write like you. Does it matter if some are upper case and others are lower case letters? What is the goal for your child? For some children it will be absolutely appropriate for them to use upper and lower case letters correctly. For other children, to expect them to use upper and lower case letters would not be appropriate. Some children will be using cursive. Again, what is the goal for your child?

I had a nine-year-old student who did not write. One day we came back from the book fair and he sat down and wrote: "I wt t th bk f" and I was able to read it out loud for him to hear, "I went to the book fair." We both went wild with excitement! I held a safe space for him in which he knew he was capable.

Once I was showing a movie to my students (ages eight to twelve) and I requested that they take notes and they did! I told them they could just write down a letter or two to remind them of what they had seen. At the end of the movie they were able to remember what they saw by reviewing their notes, and we had a wonderful discussion.

Do something different. You never know what surprise waits for you!

Using half-inch or one-inch graph paper, depending on your child's needs, to provide a point of reference from which to work is another possibility.

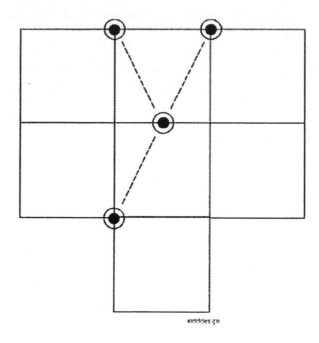

kiddies.gn

While substituting for a high school class, I met Joey who couldn't make the "y" in his name. He wanted to learn how to write it. His name wasn't complete without it. In this case, I worked with graph paper and used two squares—one above the other. On the top square I placed a dot in the upper left corner, a dot in the upper right, and a dot in the center of the bottom line. On the bottom square I placed a dot on the lower left-hand side. Now all he had to do was connect the dots with me saying out loud what he needed to do and guiding his hand as needed:

"Put the pencil point on the upper left dot, and draw a line to the dot in the center. Stop. Pick up the pencil. Put your pencil point on the upper right hand dot. Draw a line through the center dot and continue until you reach the dot at the bottom. Stop. You've made a 'y'!"

In a very short time he was putting his own dots on the graph paper. Then he was writing the "y" without placing any dots on the graph paper. Finally, he was able to write a "y" without using graph paper. I was there for a month so I was able to see this process through. This eighteen-year-old boy was finally able to write his name by himself because I held him capable, recognized he wanted to do it, and knew that between the two of us we would find a way.

Here are other suggestions:

- Use lined paper with a different colored line in the middle of the top and bottom lines.

- Have paper with textured lines so your child can feel the top and bottom lines.

- "Write" on your child's back with your finger or on the palm of her hand. Then have her do the same to you. Have her "write" in the sand, on sandpaper, in salt, in the air.

- When your child is learning to write, use verbal cues, point, and guide her movements as necessary. Whether she is tracing or writing without tracing, talk her through the process. Then have her say the process out loud also. For example, if she is learning to write the lower case "d" and has never written this letter before, you might do as I suggest below, with you doing all the writing (modeling) and her watching. Then you might have her hold the pencil and you can gently guide her hand through the entire process. Once you see she is getting the idea, you can guide as necessary.

For younger children, instead of saying they're making a line, I will say they're making a train track and as they're drawing the line I will say, "Toot, toot!" or "chug-a, chug-a, chug-a." Make it fun. Say, "Put your pencil point on the top line. Come straight down the track—toot, toot—until you touch the bottom line. Great! Now go back up the track to the middle of the line." Point to the spot and say, "Stop!" when she gets to that point.

Tell her, "Continue going around and around until you touch this bottom point." Gently move her pencil in the correct direction. Remember, you don't want her to go in the wrong direction and get her "d's" and "b's" confused. Point to the end spot and when she gets there say, "Stop! You have made a 'd'!"

Show excitement throughout the writing process. Relax and enjoy your child. It's fun pretending to be a train on a track because when your child starts going the wrong direction or doesn't stop, you can make all sorts of crash noises and get really silly.

It isn't about being serious. It's about what works and what doesn't work.

On one occasion, the occupational therapist working with my students asked me for some ideas on how to work with them. I observed her working with the children, and she was very serious and frustrated. I noticed that one of the boys had a small stuffed animal on the table so I picked it up and started speaking in a funny voice on behalf of the stuffed animal.

"Look out!" I said. "Oh, no! Turn quick! Yes! Go up! Make a big fat belly on the 'b' and slow down because you have to make a turn." The students began to laugh, and with the laughter came relaxation. It was no longer a chore. They were learning to write with their teacher and friends. This was what they wanted.

Role-Playing

Role-playing is a fun and practical way of practicing situations that occur in our everyday lives. With role-playing we can act out anticipated scenarios. It allows the child to develop confidence in different settings. Speaking on the telephone, shaking hands with people, asking questions, and dealing with conflicts are just a few situations you can role-play.

I was asked to observe a junior high class and to give suggestions. On that particular day, the six students were sitting around the table with finger puppets practicing what to say and do when there's a fight during recess. There was very little action, and the students were yawning. I suggested to the teacher that the students get out of their chairs, move the table aside, and act out the different situations. They did, and the energy shifted immediately. The students were moving around, talking, laughing, and participating fully. The role-playing got the students actively involved physically.

The more aliveness you can bring to a learning environment the more the child will retain. The yawning was a clear sign that we needed to do something in a different way to get the message across effectively. The teacher's willingness to be flexible and adapt to the needs of the children turned this lesson into a wonderful learning experience.

Mimicking

This can be very effective when your child is being disruptive. Do what he is doing and many times he will see how silly he looks or sounds and he will stop. Use humor and exaggerate his actions and sounds. Use the mirror. Let him see how he looks. Please be observant when doing this. For some children this may have the opposite effect. The child may become more agitated, more frustrated. If that's the case, stop immediately.

Changing the Mood

When you make a physical change in the room, you can also change the mood of the people in the room. Here are some simple things you can do:

- Dim the lights
- Make the lights brighter
- Bring down the blinds
- Play soft music
- Play loud music
- Put on jazz, classical, pop
- Move the furniture
- Sit on the floor

When my students were wound up, I would put their mats on the floor, dim the lights, and put on soft music. They would lie down voluntarily. I created a relaxing environment for them and they responded positively to it.

Change the mood with your voice:

- Speak in a whisper
- Stop speaking
- Speak in a funny voice
- Speak in a whinny voice

Speak with great expression, as though you are an announcer. For example, say, "Sharon is heading into the living room to recite her poem. A hush has come over the room. The audience is waiting with great anticipation! Yes, she is here and the crowd goes wild!" Everyone in the living room will probably start clapping and howling with joy. That can be a wonderful shift in mood from, "Okay kids, come and sit down. Sharon is going to rehearse her poem."

Give your child the opportunity to change the mood in the room. By experimenting, your child will learn what she needs to calm down and what she needs to get focused.

Laughter

It is important for your child to be around spontaneous laughter.

I used to take my seven-year-old student who had severe developmental disabilities, cerebral palsy, and was blind to my home. We would play games and he would laugh. He would play with my dogs and he would laugh. One day I took him to the park and put him on the swing. There were a few other children in the park around his age. When they started to laugh and giggle, he started to laugh, too. What was so amazing is that I'd never heard him so gleeful, so joyful. This laughter was different in a wonderful way. Have you had this experience with your child?

Art in Your Home

Children have wonderful imaginations. Always have miscellaneous art supplies on hand for your child to use, such as:

thread	keys
scrap paper	cardboard
egg cartons	cotton balls
construction paper	pipe cleaners
safe scissors	tape
crayons	glue
buttons	empty boxes

Decide where you want to store this stuff and when your child will have access to it. What works best for you and your child? I still keep a large plastic table cloth in my home for those occasions when friends bring their young children to the house. I want them to have an environment in which they can play, and I don't have to worry about my table top.

Using Sign Language

Children enjoy using sign language. For some children it's another way to use their bodies and for other children it's a necessity. You can pick up a sign language book in a bookstore. The words are in alphabetical order. When I worked at the elementary school, I would go into the general education classrooms and teach enough sign language to sing *Old MacDonald Had a Farm*. It was great fun signing E-I-E-I-O and then the animal signs.

If your child uses sign language, doing an activity with all the students in the class is a fun way to take the mystery out of sign language. It also allows the other students in the class and in the school to see your child in a new and positive way. They will see your child as capable and capable of doing something that perhaps they don't know how to do. I used to walk my students down the hall using sign language. They got a great kick out of playing this "game" and the other students got to see them in a different light.

Identifying Body Parts

- Play *Simon Says* to point out parts of the body.
- Make up silly songs with body parts.
- Outline your child's body on a large sheet of paper. Have her cut it out, color it, and hang it in her room.
- Put a large sheet of paper on the floor. Paint the bottom of your child's feet and have him make footprints on the paper. Do the same with his hands. Do his elbows. Be silly!

Teaching Colors

- Say the name of the color, make hand gestures, make high and low sounds, say a word that rhymes with the name of the color.

- Create a book, a treasure chest, or a collage for each color.
- Focus on one color at a time: green grapes, green pen, green leaf, green lizard, green jar, green button, green shoe, green frog. The only limit is your imagination.
- Have them wear clothing with the color they are learning.

Working with Shapes

Focus on one shape at a time. Cut out the shape, identify it, and make a picture with construction paper using only that one shape. Cut out the shape from magazine pages and then paste them onto construction paper. Your child will have a wonderful, colorful collage. Use as many details as possible when describing the shape, such as, "There are four straight lines. There are four points. There are four sides. Are all the sides the same length?" Point out the shape in your house, in a store, outside.

Combination Locks

Have you assumed that your child *will never* learn to use a combination lock? Have you assumed that your child *will* learn how to use a combination lock? I don't know if your child will or will not learn to use one, and I can tell you that many children do learn to use these locks.

When I taught children to use a combination lock, I made a model lock out of two cardboard circles that were fastened in the center for movement. The bottom circle was approximately 18" in diameter and I wrote the numbers around the outside. Then I made another circle with an arrow to point to the numbers. The children learned to move the upper circle to the right, then to the left, and then to the right again. They learned to point the arrow at specific numbers. Step-by-step they learned how to use a combination lock.

Using this type of lock will not be appropriate for all children. However, for others, by the time they go to middle school or high school, they will be able to open a combination lock.

Computer Games

Make sure the computer games your child plays fit his needs so that he doesn't become frustrated. When there is a sequencing task, is the sequencing shown horizontally and then does he have to do the sequencing vertically? If yes, maybe he doesn't have the necessary skills to transfer that information; therefore, he won't be successful. If there is sound and/or music, is it distracting or agitating to your child, or is it soothing, exciting, and motivating? If there is a "voice," is it intelligible or garbled? Watch your child playing the games. You will pick up what's working and what's not working.

A six-year-old student of mine who had severe developmental disabilities and was deaf enjoyed using the computer. He loved colors and would make beautiful designs. Every time he made a new design his face would light up and he would raise his arms in the air.

Gross Motor Skills

Teach walking up and down the stairs with alternate feet. When she's walking down the stairs, lightly tap the foot she's supposed to move to go to the next step or tap her thigh. Then tap the other foot and have her move. Repeat. She will learn to alternate her feet while walking up and down the stairs and will be very proud of this accomplishment.

Use your imagination. Here are some examples of simple exercises that you can make into games:

- Stand on one foot for one second, then two seconds, and then three seconds.
- Tiptoe forward three steps. Tiptoe backward one step.
- Hop, skip, and run.
- Run around the tree.
- Walk up and down stairs holding the railing.
- Walk up and down stairs without holding the railing when appropriate.

Guessing Games

- Describe someone in the room by hair color, length of hair, eye color, clothing.
- Describe an item in the room.
- Guess the sound: telephone ringing, doorbell, alarm on clock, washing machine, knock on the door.
- Guess the outside sounds: car door closing, someone running, bird singing, ambulance siren.

Expectations

I heard it said once that we have expectations to justify the upset we are going to have. That statement has stuck with me through the years. The words are so simple on the surface, "I expect," and yet I feel I must tread lightly. It gets tricky for me because the word *expectation* has different meanings for different people. I have personally taken pride in saying that whenever I've held high expectations for my students they have thrived in working toward those goals. Many times they not only met those expectations, they exceeded them. So if we retain *expectations* as part of our vocabulary, I would recommend that we keep our expectations high and not out of reach. By working with your child, you will get to know the difference between the two.

Consistency is an important piece of the puzzle that allows a child to thrive, to meet a goal, or any expectation. A major part of creating a safe environment for children is based on consistency. They know that you are not there to scream at them, to shame them, or to embarrass them. You are there to assist them in reaching a goal. They also know you have expectations surrounding their behavior, and if they haven't performed to an expectation there will be consequences. Children need us to be consistent.

After playing around with the word *expectations—when* I use it, *how* I use it, *why* I use it—I'm more comfortable with it. I realize the process of having expectations comes from my being grounded in the belief that the child is capable, that the child wants to learn, and that together we will make a difference. Coming from this belief system makes it easy and natural for me to shift gears and to do something different when I know what I've done isn't working.

When the school year started, one of the six-year-old students in my class would come into the room and proceed to wipe everything off the tabletop with one big swipe of his arm and I mean <u>everything</u>. I was not going to rearrange the entire room for this child until I was convinced that he couldn't control his behavior. Each time this happened, he was reminded that he was responsible for the mess, and he was responsible for cleaning it up. Then he would put everything back on the table. After four or five times, he never threw anything off the table again.

This same child would walk down the hall screaming. Every time he started to scream, he would be walked back to the room and start again. He learned very quickly that if he didn't stop screaming he was not going to gym, music, art, or recess. He stopped screaming.

Be grounded in knowing that
your child is capable
and <u>wants to learn</u>.
Together you will make a difference.

Conclusion

Let me share a couple more stories about the young boy who had severe developmental disabilities, cerebral palsy, and was blind.

One day, his mother came to thank me for teaching her young son how to hug. She told me that since he had started hugging his two sisters they were now relating to him as a little boy, which they had not done before. All of a sudden he became a real part of their family—a participant, a little boy. She was so grateful for this simple and one of our most cherished acts of affection.

At the time, when I was playing with him, I would hug him and then I'd have him hug me back. I was not thinking about the far-reaching effects of this activity; I just did it. I did not think about how it would touch another person's life or how it would touch a family. That accomplishment, the movement of taking another person into your arms and holding tightly had changed a family. A gift was given to his family that words can not adequately express. The lesson in this for me was to continue finding ways to create successes because we never know the wonderful ripple effect it might have.

LHALL '04

Besides spending time with this young boy in the classroom we were also privileged to have him live with us for a month. Being grounded in the knowledge that he was capable and wanted to learn allowed me to be playful with this child and to experiment with different situations and experiences. He learned to sit on a tricycle with the use of some Velcro, to hold the handlebars, and to move his legs on the pedals while someone pushed him. He learned to sit on a swing and hold on while someone pushed him. He learned to move about the room on a crawler that I built. He learned to feed himself and to throw a ball.

He loved classical music and Willie Nelson and would move his arms and "sing" with glee. He loved hearing the Itsy Bitsy Spider song and would laugh every time someone sang it. He loved saying, "HO, HO, HO!" and would laugh when I joined in. He loved sleeping with my dogs. He loved getting a massage. He loved the feel of a leaf tickling the palm of his hand.

These are only a few of the simple pleasures he enjoyed, and I loved bringing them into his life to share with him.

My wish is for all children to have the freedom to express themselves with vitality, to have love in their lives, and to celebrate life fully. Adults, give yourselves permission to laugh and play. Enjoy the magnificence of your child and savor the simple successes!

Printed in the United States
54527LVS00002B/30